Numbers and the Number System

PUBLISHED BY THE PRESS SYNDICATE OF THE UNIVERSITY OF CAMBRIDGE
The Pitt Building, Trumpington Street, Cambridge, United Kindgom

CAMBRIDGE UNIVERSITY PRESS
The Edinburgh Building, Cambridge CB2 2RU, UK
40 West 20th Street, New York, NY 10011-4211, USA
477 Williamstown Road, Port Melbourne, VIC 3207, Australia
Ruiz de Alarcón 13, 28014 Madrid, Spain
Dock House, The Waterfront, Cape Town 8001, South Africa

http://www.cambridge.org

© Cambridge University Press 2001

First published 2001
Reprinted 2002

Printed in Italy by G. Canale & C. S.p.A. - Borgaro T.se (Turin)

Typefaces Frutiger, Helvetica, Minion, Swift *System* QuarkXPress 4.03

A catalogue record for this book is available from the British Library

ISBN 0 521 78478 6 paperback

Text illustration Adam Stower

General editors for Cambridge Mathematics Direct
Sandy Cowling, Jane Crowden, Andrew King, Jeanette Mumford

Writing team for Numbers and the Number System 5
Elaine Kilner, Andrew King, Sandra Leggett, Jeanette Mumford, Mary Nathan,
Chris Sharples, Elizabeth Toohig, Allison Toogood, Cathy Tracey

The writers and publishers would like to thank the many schools and individuals
who trialled lessons for Cambridge Mathematics Direct.

NOTICE TO TEACHERS
It is illegal to reproduce any part of this work in material form (including photocopying and electronic storage)
except under the following circumstances:
(i) where you are abiding by a licence granted to your school or institution by the Copyright Licensing Agency;
(ii) where no such licence exists, or where you wish to exceed the terms of a licence, and you have
gained the written permission of Cambridge University Press;
(iii) where you are allowed to reproduce without permission under the provisions of Chapter 3 of
the Copyright, Designs and Patents Act 1988.

Abbreviations and symbols
IP   Interactive picture
CM   Copymaster
A   is practice work
B   develops ideas
C   is extension work
★   if needed, helps with work in A
A red margin indicates that the children work with the teacher.
A green margin indicates that children work independently.

Contents

Place value (PV) Place value, ordering and rounding

PV1 **Counting**
PV1.1 Reading and writing big numbers — 5
PV1.2 Generating numbers — 7
PV1.3 Ordering large numbers — 9
PV1.4 Above and below zero — 10

PV2 **Estimation and approximation**
PV2.1 Estimating quantities and proportions — 12
PV2.2 Estimating and rounding 4-digit numbers — 14
PV2.3 Estimating and rounding measurements — 16

PV3 **Multiplication and division by 100**
PV3.1 Multiplying by 10 and 100 — 17
PV3.2 Dividing by 100 — 18
PV3.3 Using a calculator for multiplication and division — 19

Numbers (N): Properties of numbers and number sequences

N1 **Recognising odds/evens/squares/multiples/factors**
N1.2 Square numbers 2 — 20
N1.3 Odd and even numbers — 22
N1.5 Divisibility — 23

N2 **Steps and multiples**
N2.1 Sequences and patterns — 24
N2.2 Sequences with 2-digit steps — 26
N2.3 Multiples and factors — 28
N2.4 Pairs of factors — 30
N2.5 Multiples of more than 1 number — 32

N 3 **Reasoning about numbers**
N3.1 Making general statements — 34
N3.2 Patterns and puzzles — 36
N3.3 Factor puzzles — 38
N3.4 Patterns and sequences — 40
N3.5 Finding and using the rule — 42

Fractions (F): Fractions, decimals and percentages, ratio and proportion

F1	**Equivalent fractions**	
F1.1	Equivalent fractions	44
F1.2	Thirds, sixths, ninths	46
F1.4	Tenths and hundredths	48
F1.5	Improper fractions	51
F2	**Decimal fractions**	
F2.1	Introducing hundredths	54
F2.2	Ordering decimals	55
F2.4	Changing units	57
F3	**Equivalence between decimals and fractions**	
F3.1	Finding equivalents	59
F3.2	Calculator fractions	60
F3.3	Decimals for money and length	61
F4	**Ordering fractions**	
F4.1	Comparing fractions	63
F4.2	Ordering fractions	64
F4.3	Ordering decimals	65
F5	**Fractions of quantities**	
F5.1	Fractions and division 1	66
F5.2	Fractions and division 2	68
F5.3	Problems involving proportion	70
F5.4	Quotients and fractions	72
F5.5	Quotients and decimals	73
F6	**Percentages**	
F6.1	Introducing percentages	74
F6.2	Percentages of a shape	75
F6.3	Percentages, fractions and decimals	77
F6.4	Percentage problems	79

V1.1 Reading and writing big numbers

> **Key idea** Each place in a number has a value 10 times bigger than the one to its right.

A1 Work with a partner.

You need a set of 0–9 digit cards between you.

Player A
Take 3 cards and make the biggest number you can.
Read this number in words to Player B.

Player B
Write it down in figures.

Check to see that your numbers are the same.

Both write the number in words.

Now do everything again taking 4 cards, then 5, then 6.

B1 How big are the planets in the solar system?
Multiply by 10 to find out.

Planet	Distance through the centre in km	Numeral	Words
Pluto	230 x 10	2300	Two thousand three hundred
Mercury	488 x 10		
Mars	679 x 10		
Venus	1210 x 10		
Earth	1276 x 10		
Neptune	4950 x 10		
Uranus	5100 x 10		
Saturn	11 999 x 10		
Jupiter	14 280 x 10		

PV1 Counting

C1 The table shows the distance of some of Jupiter's moons from Jupiter.

Moon	Distance in km
Amalthea	180 000
Thebe	222 000
Io	422 000
Europa	670 000
Ganymede	1 070 000
Leda	11 100 000
Ananke	21 200 000

You need place value cards and dice.

- Pick a hundreds, tens and units card at random to make a 3-digit number.
- Throw the dice. This tells you how many times to multiply your number by 10.

Your space probe can travel this far from Jupiter. Which moon can it visit?

Try to visit all these moons!

Key idea | Each place in a number has a value 10 times bigger than the one to its right.

PV1 Counting

PV1.2 Generating numbers

> **Key idea** It is important to know the value of each digit in a number.

A1 Make the biggest and smallest integers you can with these digits.

a 3, 1, 9, 7, 2, 5, 6   b 4, 0, 8, 2, 5, 7, 3   c 5, 8, 0, 6, 0, 1, 4

A2 You need a calculator.

Key this into your calculator. [C] [9] [9] [8] [+] [+] [=] [0]

Enter the starting number.

Write the first 6 numbers in these sequences.

a 1000, 1998, 2996, ____, ____, ____

b 5000, 5998, ____, ____, ____, ____

c 10 000, 10 998, ____, ____, ____, ____

d 19 000, ____, ____, ____, ____, ____

PV1 Counting

B1 Write what you need to add to 31 658 to make your calculator show:

a 31758   b 32658   c 31659
d 41658   e 31668

B2 Write what you need to subtract from 76 487 to make your calculator show:

a 75487   b 76477   c 76480
d 76287   e 66487

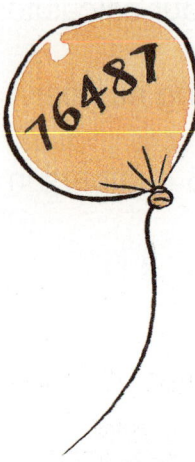

B3 Do CM 1.

C1 You have a 6-spike abacus and 5 beads.

You can only use the 3 left-hand spikes.

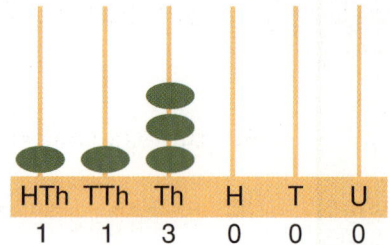

Using these 3 columns and all 5 beads, you can make 15 different 6-digit numbers.

True or false? Investigate.

C2 If you start with 100 000 on your calculator and subtract 999 one hundred times you end up with 100. Why?

> **Key idea** It is important to know the value of each digit in a number.

PV1 Counting

PV1.3 Ordering large numbers

Key idea | To put numbers in order correctly we need to know the value of the digits in them.

A1 nails 11 428   screws 8924   nuts 18 248   bolts 15 824   washers 108 592   tacks 9482

Write these numbers

a in ascending order

b in descending order

A2 Copy these statements and use < or > to make them true.

a 14 200 ☐ 14 212

b 10 216 ☐ 10 026

c 27 257 ☐ 28 257

d 36 558 ☐ 46 558

e 55 005 ☐ 50 050

f 31 427 ☐ 31 425

B1 Write true or false for each of these statements.

a 314 400 > 314 300

b 942 019 < 942 109

c 304 519 < 314 109

d 924 910 > 942 019

B2 Use jottings and write the number that is half way between:

a 17 700 and 17 900

b 26 200 and 27 000

c 33 300 and 34 300

d 42 716 and 42 796

B3 a Write 5 true statements for   14 270 ≤ ☐ ≤ 14 520

b Write 5 true statements for   25 840 ≥ ☐ ≥ 25 740

B4 Write these integers in order, least first.

a −5, −2, −8, −1, 0, 5, −6

b −7, −3, 3, −4, −9, 2

PV1 Counting

PV1.4 Above and below zero

Key idea: Positive and negative numbers grow out from zero.

A1

a Program your calculator to subtract 1.

b Press [2]

c Press [=] 6 times.

d Write down the sequence of numbers. 2, 1, 0, ☐, ☐, ☐, ☐

A2 Repeat the steps in A1 for each of these programs.

a Press [C][3][−][−][=][0]
Press [4]

b Press [C][4][−][−][=][0]
Press [6]

c Press [C][5][−][−][=][0]
Press [5]

d Press [C][10][−][−][=][ ]
Press [2][3]

A3 These temperatures were recorded during a week in January. Copy and complete the table.

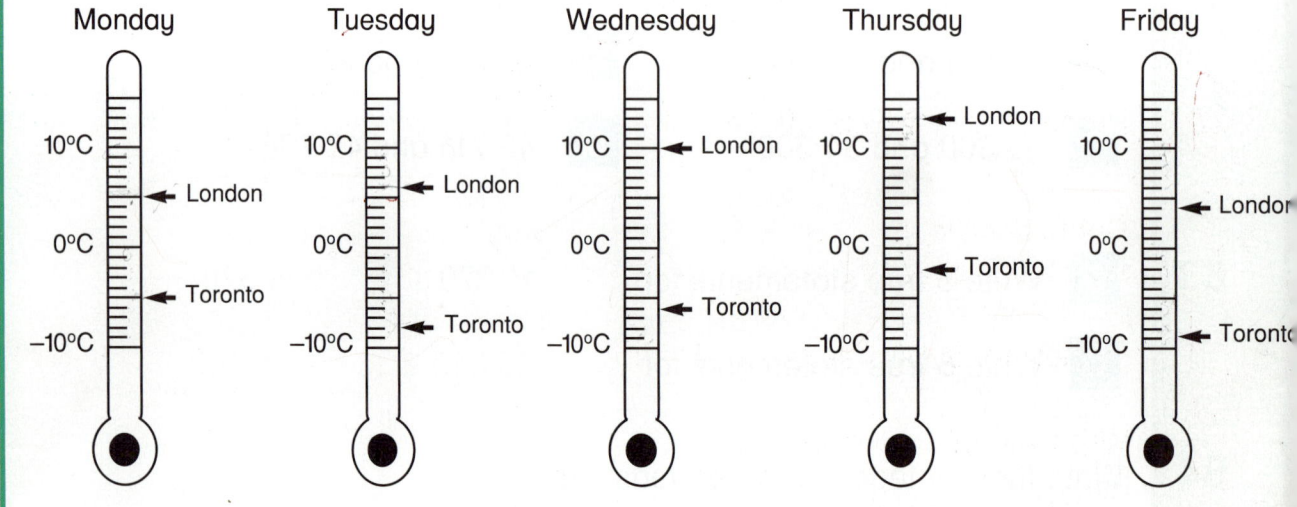

City	Monday	Tuesday	Wednesday	Thursday	Friday
London	5°C				
Toronto					

10 PV1 Counting

B1 Copy and complete:

a) 8, 5, ☐, –1, ☐, ☐

b) 22, 13, 4, ☐, ☐, ☐

c) –21, –18, ☐, ☐, ☐, ☐

d) ☐, ☐, 3, 0, –3, ☐, ☐

B2 Make these statements true. Choose < or >.

a) –4°C ☐ 4°C

b) 2°C ☐ –3°C

c) –12°C ☐ –3°C

d) –6°C ☐ 0°C

B3 Look at the thermometers in A3.

Work out the difference between the temperatures in London and Toronto for each day.

B4 Work out the temperature on Saturday for both cities.

Toronto fell by 7°C, London rose by 8°C from Friday.

B5 How many degrees warmer was London than Toronto on Saturday?

C1 Design calculator programs to subtract 5, 6 and 7.

Choose your starting number.

Write the first 10 integers in your sequences.

C2 Program your calculator to subtract 2.

Count the steps from 20°C to –20°C.

Repeat for subtracting 4, 5, 10, 20.

Write what you notice.

Start	Subtract	Number of steps	Finish
20°C	2		–20°C
	4		
	5		
	10		
	20		

Key idea Positive and negative numbers grow out from zero.

PV1 Counting

PV2.1 Estimating quantities and proportions

> **Key idea** You can use what you know about fractions to help estimate parts of a quantity.

A1 Estimate the proportion of pasta in each jar.

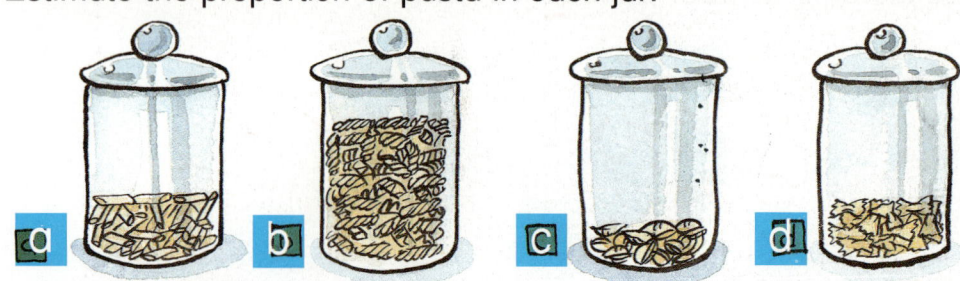

A2 Billy Bragg is 9 years old. Which of his statements could be true?

Estimate and check.

Write each sentence in your book and put a ✓ or ✗.

- a I am nearly 2 m tall.
- b My thumb is about 50 mm long.
- c I can type 75 words in one minute.
- d I can jump 300 mm into the air.

B1 You need coins.

Estimate, then count exactly, how many of each value of coin will fit along a 30 cm ruler and a 1 metre straight line.

Copy and complete the table.

Value of coin	30 cm ruler estimate	30 cm ruler count	1 m line estimate	1 m line count
1p				
2p				
5p				
10p				
£1				

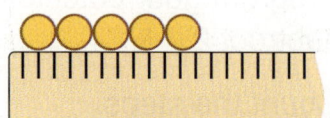

B2 You need coins of the same value.

Estimate the height of a stack

- a 10 coins tall
- b 100 coins tall

12 PV2 Estimation and approximation

C1 The diagram shows the number of bricks needed to build 1 square metre of wall.

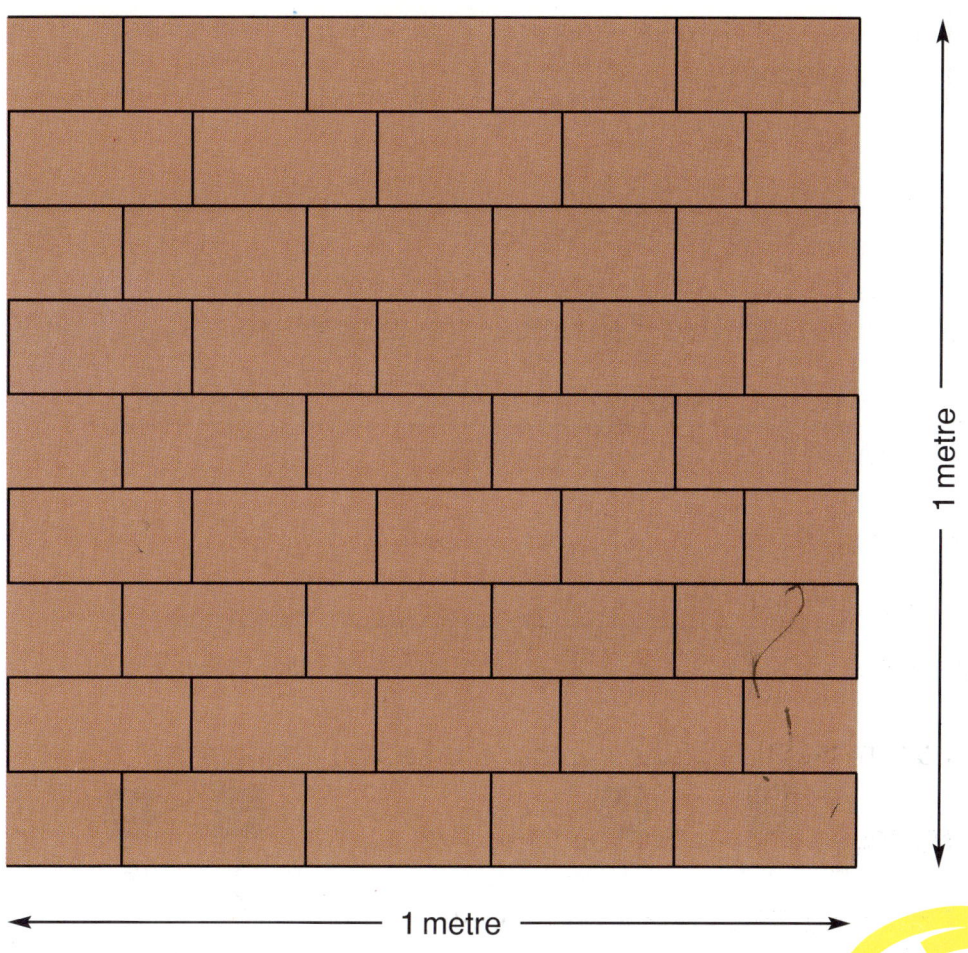

What about half bricks?

Estimate, then calculate, the number of bricks in 1 square metre of wall.

a estimate ☐ bricks **b** calculate ☐ bricks

C2 Estimate, then work out the number of bricks for these walls.

a 2 m high by 1 m long **b** 2 m high by 2 m long
c 3 m high by 3 m long **d** 2 m high by 4 m long
e 3 m high by 6 m long **f** 3 m high by 10 m long

Key idea You can use what you know about fractions to help estimate parts of a quantity.

PV2 Estimation and approximation

PV2.2 Estimating and rounding 4-digit numbers

Key idea | You can use what you know about rounding to help estimate answers to calculations.

A1

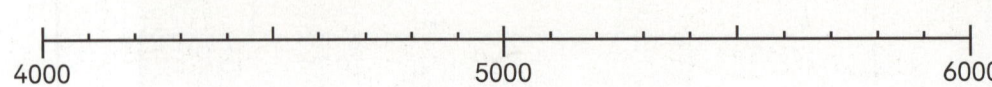

Copy and complete. Use the number line to help you.

number	nearest 10	nearest 100	nearest 1000
4217			
4683			
5325			
5754			

A2

Estimate the position of the number marked by each arrow.

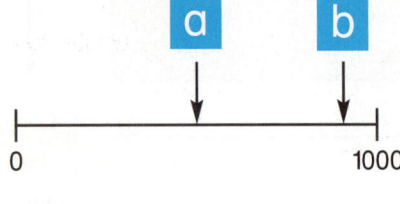
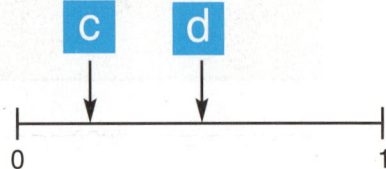
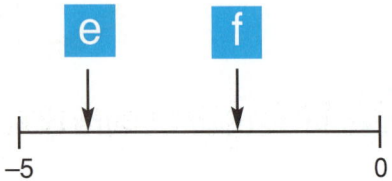
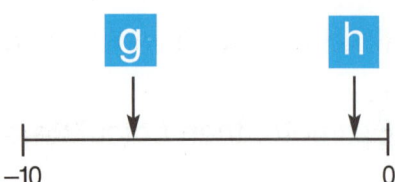

B1

Which is the best approximation for these calculations?

	calculation	approximation			
a	509 + 95	500 + 100	600 + 100	510 + 100	500 + 90
b	695 + 106	700 + 100	700 + 110	600 + 100	600 + 110
c	19 × 24	19 × 20	20 × 20	20 × 24	20 × 30
d	29 × 16	30 × 10	30 × 20	29 × 20	30 × 16

PV2 Estimation and approximation

B2 a 437 to the nearest 10 is ☐   b 1785 to the nearest 100 is ☐

c 3046 to the nearest 1000 is ☐   d 969 to the nearest 1000 is ☐

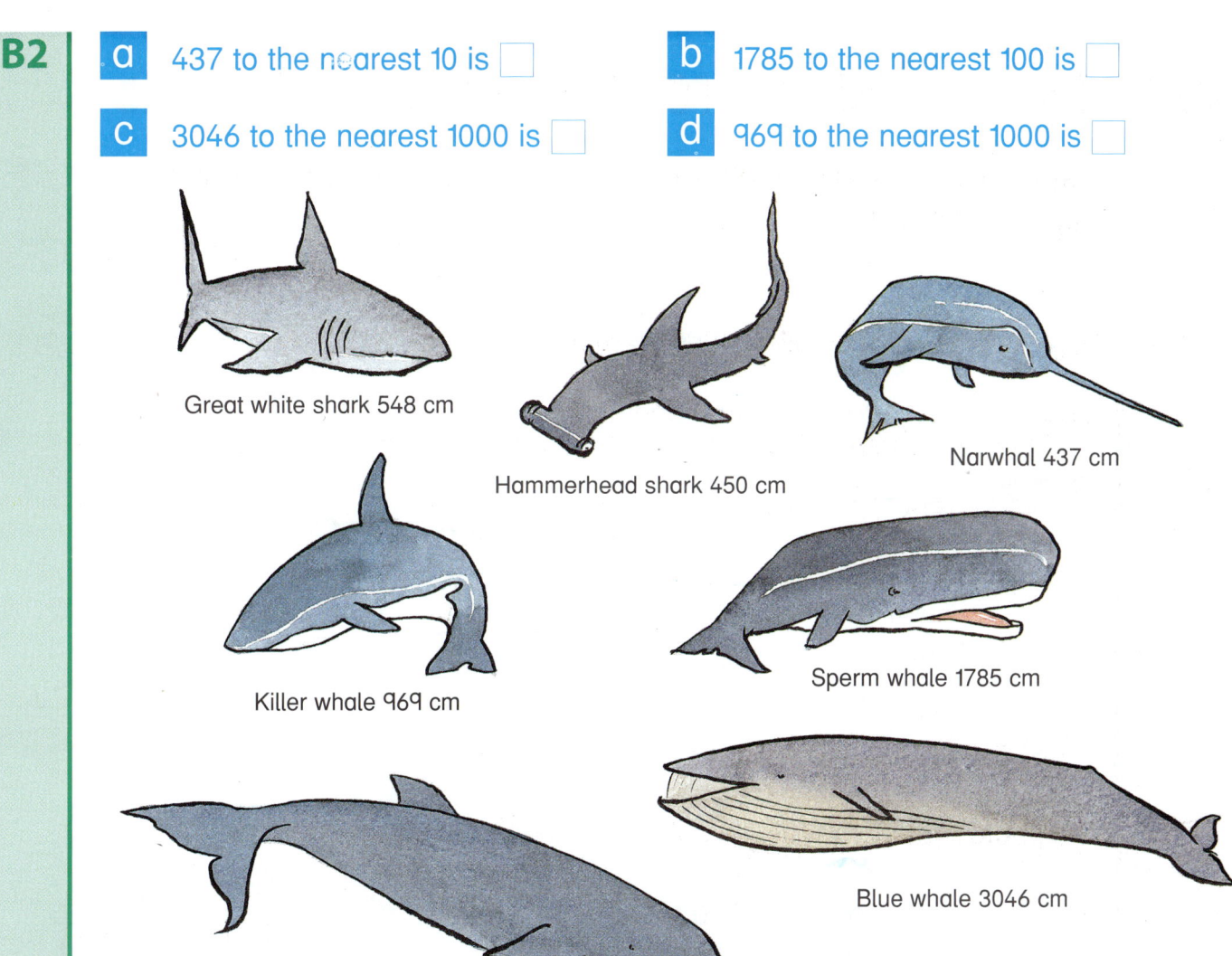

Great white shark 548 cm
Hammerhead shark 450 cm
Narwhal 437 cm
Killer whale 969 cm
Sperm whale 1785 cm
Blue whale 3046 cm
Minke whale 1033 cm

B3 Name a sea creature with a length in cm of

a 550 to the nearest 10   b 1790 to the nearest 10

c 3000 to the nearest 100   d 400 to the nearest 100

e 1000 to the nearest 1000   f 2000 to the nearest 1000

C1 List the palindromic numbers from 5005 to 5995. Round each number to the nearest 10, 100 and 1000.

Write about the patterns you notice.

Do the same for the palindromic numbers from 9009 to 9999.

Key idea You can use what you know about rounding to help estimate answers to calculations.

PV2 Estimation and approximation

15

PV2.3 Estimating and rounding measurements

> **Key idea** You can use what you know about rounding to help estimate answers to problems.

A1 Measure these lines to the nearest centimetre.

Use the ≈ sign to record the lengths.

AB ≈ 5 cm

B1 You need some lined paper.

a Draw 10 lines. Each line must
- begin and end on a printed line
- cross at least 2 printed lines.

b Measure to the nearest millimetre
- the total length of your line
- the length of each part between 2 printed lines.

c Write what you notice.

C1
a Find the perimeter of the triangle in mm.

b Round the perimeter length to the nearest cm.

c Round the length of each side to the nearest cm and total the 3 rounded lengths.

d Compare the answers for b and c and write what you notice.

33 mm, 55 mm, 46 mm

C2 Repeat the steps in C1 for this equilateral triangle.

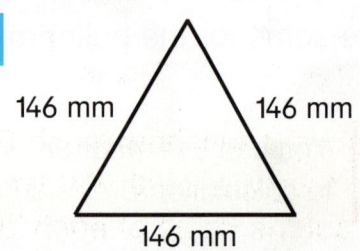

146 mm, 146 mm, 146 mm

16 PV2 Estimation and approximation

PV3.1 Multiplying by 10 and 100

> **Key idea** You can multiply by 100 by multiplying by 10 and then by 10 again.

A1 Multiply each number by 10 and then by 10 again.
Then multiply the original number by 100.

a) 40 × 10 = 400   b) 70   c) 62   d) 34

400 × 10 = ☐

40 × 100 = ☐

Use equipment if you wish.

A2 Copy and complete these patterns.

a) 4 × 100 = ☐   b) 6 × 100 = ☐   c) ☐ × 100 = 1200

40 × 100 = ☐   60 × 100 = ☐   120 × ☐ = 12 000

400 × 100 = ☐   600 × 100 = ☐   1200 × 100 = ☐

B1 Complete these sequences.

a) 16   160   1600   ☐   ☐   b) 1.8   18   ☐   1800   ☐   ☐

c) 0.9   ☐   90   900   ☐   ☐

d) Make up 2 more sequences of your own.

B2

picture £205   vase £7.25   chair £9.50   table £4.99 lamp £13.95   best china £30.70

The labels show how much Grandma paid when she bought these things.
Today they are worth 100 times as much.
Work out the value of each item.

PV3 Multiplication and division by 100

PV3.2 Dividing by 100

> **Key idea** When you divide by 10, the digits move 1 place to the right.
> When you divide by 100 they move 2 places to the right.

A1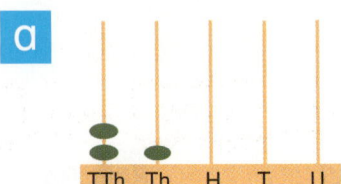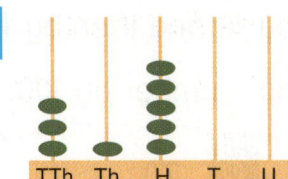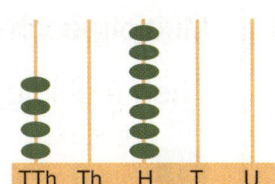

Write the number each abacus shows, divide the number by 10, and divide the number by 100.

A2 Copy and complete.

a) 600 ÷ 100 = ☐
6000 ÷ 100 = ☐
60 000 ÷ 100 = ☐

b) 900 ÷ ☐ = 9
9000 ÷ ☐ = 90
☐ ÷ 100 = 900

A3
a) 7000 ÷ 100 = ☐
b) 4600 ÷ 100 = ☐
c) 13 000 ÷ 100 = ☐
d) 53 000 ÷ 100 = ☐

B1 Copy and complete.

a) 400 000 ÷ 100 = 4000
40 000 ÷ 100 = ☐
4 000 ÷ 100 = ☐
400 ÷ 100 = ☐
40 ÷ 100 = 0.4

Complete these in the same way.

b) 600 000 ÷ 100
c) 120 000 ÷ 100
d) 390 000 ÷ 100

B2 This bag contains £250.

is the same as
How many £10 notes?
How many £1 coins?
How many 10p coins?
How many 1p coins?

B3 Do CM 7.

PV3.3 Using a calculator for multiplication & division

| Key idea | When you multiply by 10 or 100, digits move to the left. When you divide by 10 or 100, digits move to the right. |

A1 Copy and complete the number tracks.

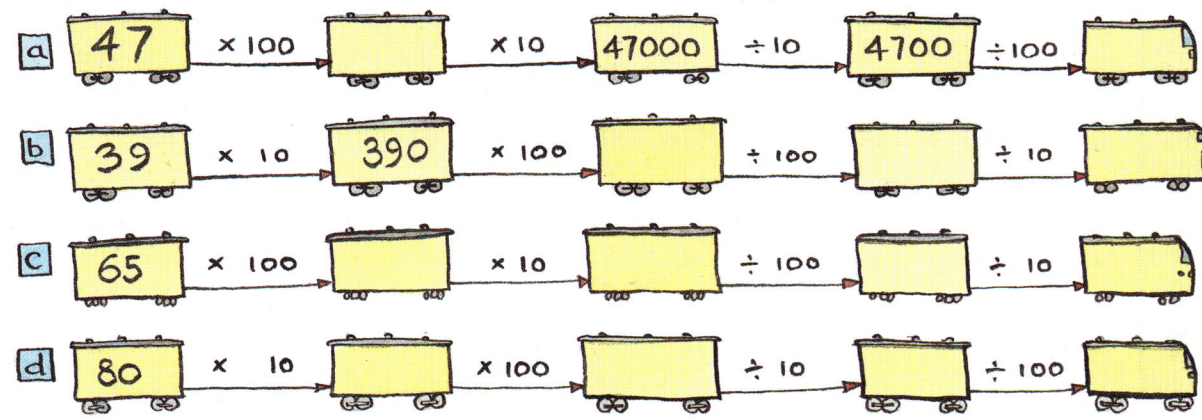

A2 Write what you notice about the first and last numbers.

A3 Do CM 9.

B1 **a** Copy and complete tracks A and B where 16 is the starting number.

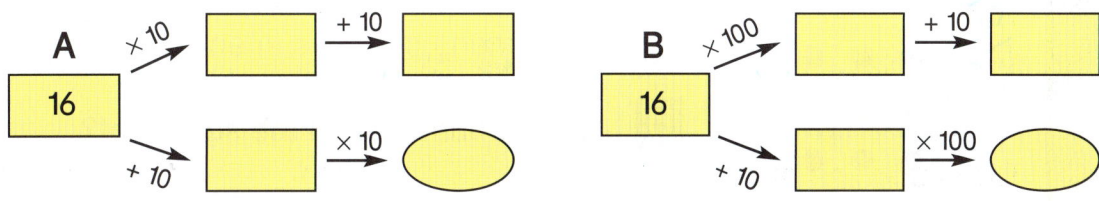

b Use the starting numbers 23 and 39 and complete tracks A and B.

c Write what you notice.

B2 **a** Copy and complete track C for the starting numbers 16, 23 and 39.

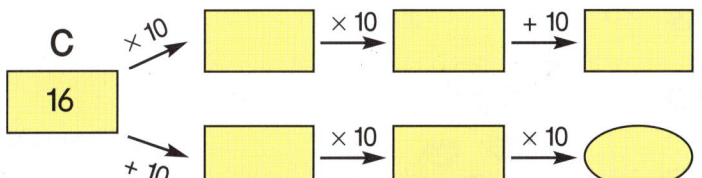

b Explain why 2 pairs of finishing numbers are the same.

B3 Use 100 as the starting number for tracks A, B and C.

C1 Using tracks A, B and C, investigate for some 3-digit and 4-digit numbers.

PV3 Multiplication and division by 10

N1.2 Square numbers 2

> **Key idea** Square numbers make a sequence.

A1

a List all the square numbers from 1 to 100 like this:

1   4   9   ...

b Write the difference between each pair of numbers like this:

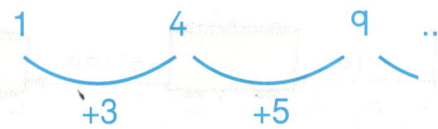

c Explain the pattern in words.

d Which is the next square number after 100?

A2 9 counters are arranged as a square.

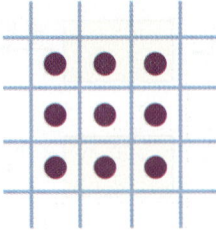

a How many counters in each row?

b Which number is 9 the square of?

A3 How many counters will be in each row if you arrange the following as squares?

a 16   **b** 4   **c** 36

d 100   **e** 25   **f** 49

Use counters if you need to.

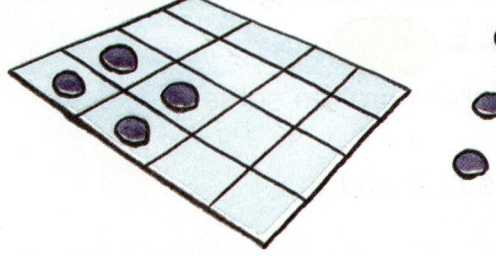
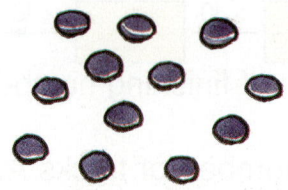
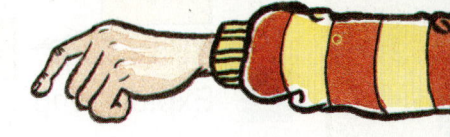

N1 Recognising odd/evens/squares/multiples/factors

B1 What is

a 3^2? b 2^2? c 8^2? d 5^2?

e 10^2? f 9^2? g 1^2? h 7^2?

B2 a Look for patterns and discuss with your teacher.

$1 = 1 = 1 \times 1 = 1^2$

$1 + 3 = 4 = 2 \times 2 = 2^2$

$1 + 3 + 5 = 9 = 3 \times 3 = 3^2$

b Complete the next 3 lines of the sequence in your book.

c What do you think the sum of the first 10 odd numbers will be? Give a reason for your answer.

C1 Here is a sequence of shapes.

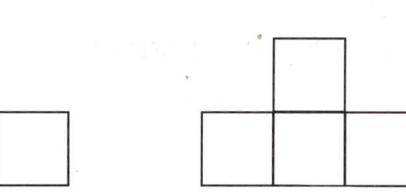 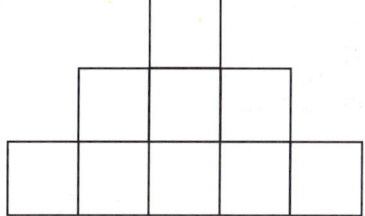

a What do you notice about the rows of squares in each shape?

b What do you notice about the total number of squares in each shape?

c Draw the next 3 shapes in the sequence.

d Look for a simple way to turn each of your drawings into a square. Explain your method.

Key idea | Square numbers make a sequence.

N1 Recognising odd/evens/squares/multiples/factors

21

N1.3 Odd and even numbers

> **Key idea** It is useful to know what happens when you calculate with odd and even numbers.

A1
- **a** Write down 3 even numbers between 15 and 25.
- **b** Find the sum of your numbers. Is it even or odd?
- **c** Repeat for two more sets of 3 even numbers.
  What do you notice about the totals?
- **d** Write down 4 even numbers greater than 15 and find their sum.
  Is it even or odd?
- **e** Repeat for two more sets of 4 even numbers.
  What do you notice about the totals?
- **f** Write a sentence about the sum of even numbers.

A2

- **a** Choose 1 odd and 1 even number from the list and find their difference.
- **b** Repeat **a** with a different pair of numbers.
- **c** Write a sentence about the difference between an odd and an even number.
- **d** Now choose 2 odd numbers from the list and find their difference.
- **e** Repeat **d** with a different pair of numbers.
- **f** Write a sentence about the difference between odd numbers.

C1 Try to make all the numbers from 1 to 20 by adding consecutive numbers.

For example, 12 can be made like this: $3 + 4 + 5 = 12$

Use as many consecutive numbers as you like.

N1.5 Divisibility

> **Key idea** Look at the last digits to identify multiples of 2, 4, 5, 10 and 100.

B1 Which of these numbers are divisible by 100?

908 500 620

7060 8700

17 250 31 000 64 900

C1 **a** Draw a Venn diagram in your book.

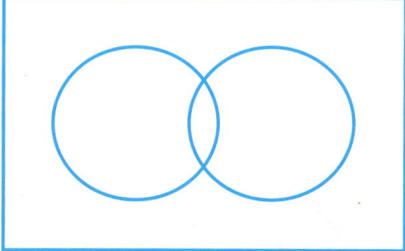

b Label the circles 'is a multiple of 2' and 'is a multiple of 5'.

c Record these numbers in the correct section:

28 45 1 125 20 827

910 5 315 121 96 30

d What do you notice about those numbers that are multiples of both 2 and 5?

e Where would you put multiples of 100 on your Venn diagram? Why?

f Where would you put multiples of 20 on your Venn diagram? Why?

N1 Recognising odds/evens/squares/multiples/factors   23

N2.1 Sequences and patterns

> **Key idea** You can continue a number sequence when you know the size of the step and which way to count.

A1 Copy and complete the number sequences.

a 7 14 21 ☐ ☐ ☐ ☐ ☐ ☐ 70

b 6 12 ☐ 24 ☐ ☐ ☐ ☐ ☐ 60

c 15 10 5 ☐ –5 ☐ ☐ ☐ ☐ –30

d –48 –40 ☐ ☐ ☐ ☐ ☐ ☐ 16 ☐

e –62 –54 ☐ ☐ –36 ☐ ☐ ☐ ☐ ☐

A2 You need some counters.

- Choose a small number to make a starting pattern.
- Choose a single-digit number to add each time.

Example

3 → 5 → 7

+ 2   + 2

- Draw and write down your pattern.

B1 Write the next 4 numbers in each sequence.

Write a rule. For example, add 2 each time.

Use number lines to help.

a 4, 7, 10, …

b 7, 12, 17, …

c 48, 39, 30, …

d 16, 9, 2, …

e –23, –29, –35, …

f –65, –57, –49, …

B2 Draw the next 3 diagrams in each pattern.
Write the rule.

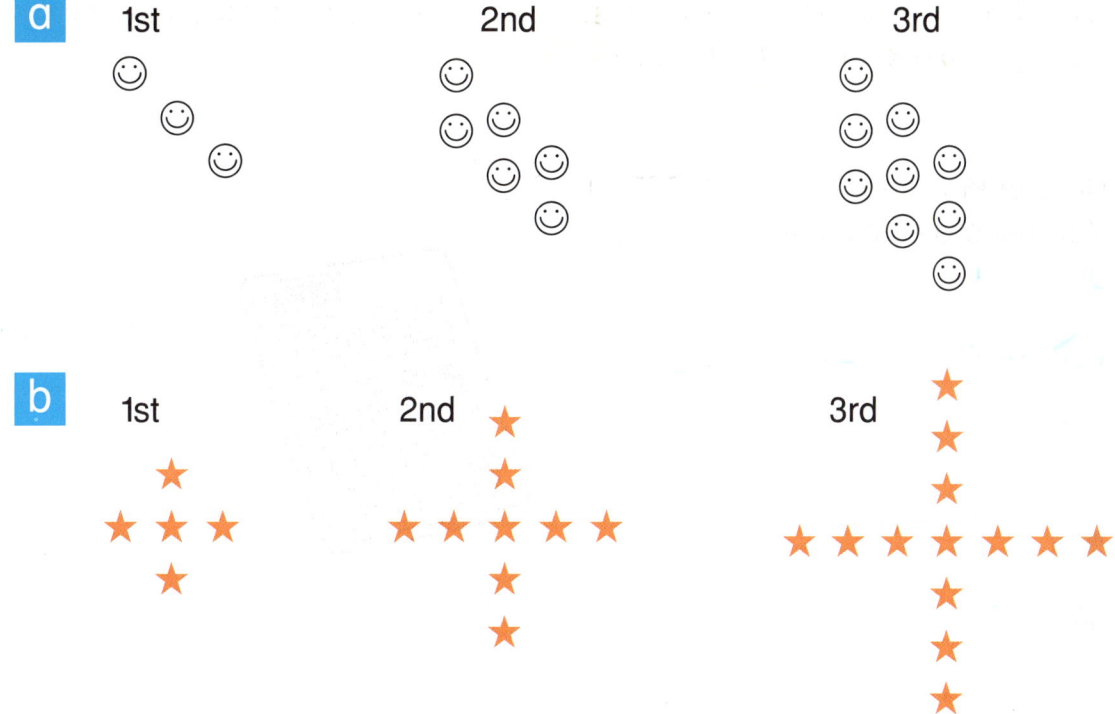

C1 Look at each pattern in B2.

Find how many in the 10th and 100th diagrams.

C2 Make up your own pattern like the patterns in B2.

Find how many are in the 10th and 100th diagrams.

Key idea You can continue a number sequence when you know the size of the step and which way to count.

N2 Steps and multiples

N 2.2 Sequences with 2-digit steps

Key idea | To find missing numbers in a sequence, first write the difference between each next-door pair of numbers.

A1 Do CM 16.
You need a calculator.

A2 Find the next 3 numbers in each of these sequences.

a 1 12 23 ☐ ☐ ☐

b 13 26 39 ☐ ☐ ☐

c 100 89 78 ☐ ☐ ☐

d 145 130 115 ☐ ☐ ☐

A3 Write the number that is missing from each sequence.

a 77 88 99 ☐ 121

b 105 84 ☐ 42 21

c 19 38 ☐ 76 95

d 225 ☐ 175 150 125

B1 Write the next 4 numbers in each sequence and write the rule.

a 100 121 142 163 ☐ ☐ ☐ ☐ The rule is _____

b 200 185 170 155 ☐ ☐ ☐ ☐ The rule is _____

c 1 3 6 10 ☐ ☐ ☐ ☐ The rule is _____

d 1 4 9 16 ☐ ☐ ☐ ☐ The rule is _____

e –105 –84 –63 ☐ ☐ ☐ ☐ The rule is _____

Remember to use the key idea.

B2 You need a calculator.

Set the constant function for adding 21 each time. C 2 1 + + = 0

Enter 7 then press = 6 times.

Write the sequence you make.

7 28 ☐ ☐ ☐ ☐ ☐

B3 Now set the constant function for adding 19 each time.

Press = 7 times.

Write the sequence you make.

19 38 ☐ ☐ ☐ ☐ ☐

C1 Set the constant function to add 16 each time.

Write the first 9 numbers in the seqeunce you make.

C2 Reset to add 12 each time. How often must you press = to make the same finishing number as in C1? Can you explain why?

C3 Continue these sequences until you find a number that is in both of them.

a   15, 30, 45, ...   b   18, 36, 54, ...

C4 a   Which numbers between 0 and 300 are multiples of both 15 and 25?

b   Draw a Venn diagram

numbers between 0 and 300

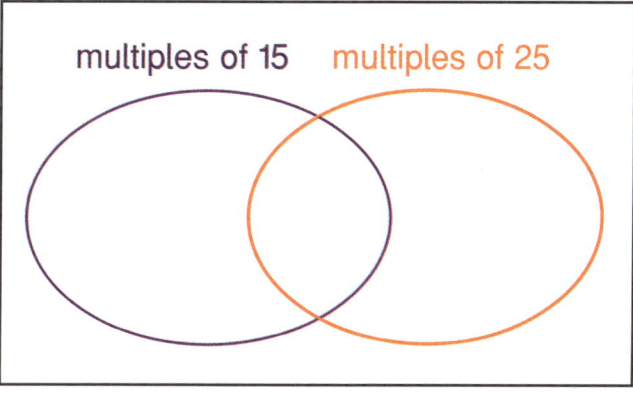

Key idea | To find missing numbers in a sequence, first write the difference between each next-door pair of numbers.

N2 Steps and multiples

N2.3 Multiples and factors

Key idea | When you know your tables, you can spot the multiples of a number quickly.

A1 You need CM 67.

Ring the numbers yellow if they are exactly divisible by 6.
red if they are exactly divisible by 8.
blue if they are exactly divisible by 9.

Draw Venn diagrams like these and sort the numbers to match their labels.

a multiples of 6   multiples of 8

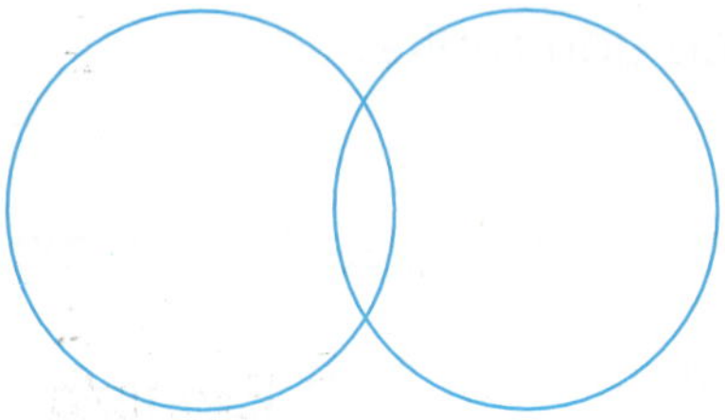

b multiples of 6   multiples of 9

A2 For each triangle

- Find the missing factor or product.
- Write 2 division sentences.
- Write 2 multiplication sentences

Example

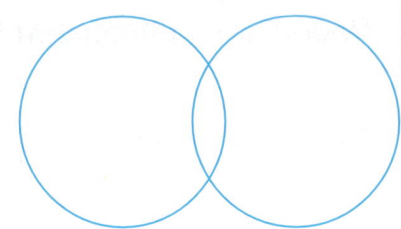

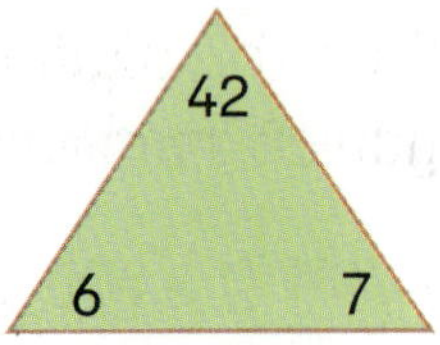

$6 \times 7 = 42$ $42 \div 6 = 7$
$7 \times 6 = 42$ $42 \div 7 = 6$

a  48, 8

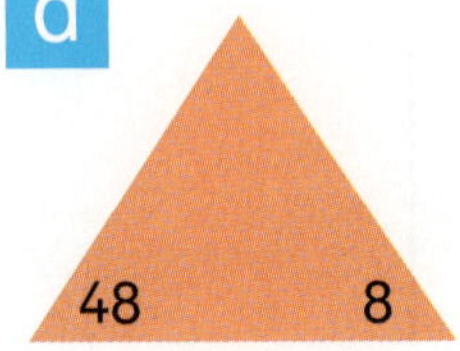

b 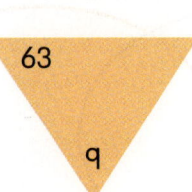 63, 9

c 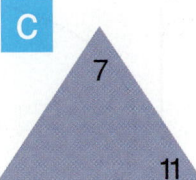 7, 11

d 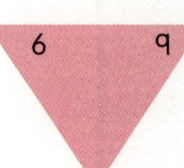 6, 9

e 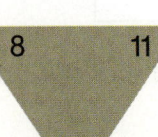 8, 11

f  35, 7

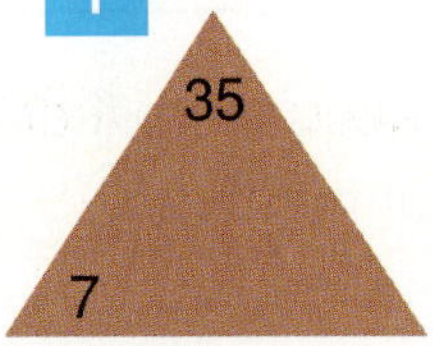

g 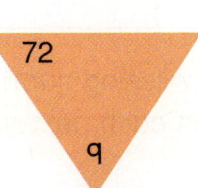 72, 9

h 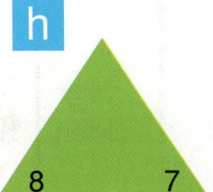 8, 7

B1

● ● ● ● ○ ○ ○ ● ● ● ● ○ ○ ○ ● ● ● ● ○ ○ ○

a What is the rule?

b What colour is the 23rd counter?

Use what you know about multiples of 7 to help you

c What colour is the 54th counter   54 ÷ 7 = 7
7 × 7 = 49 = 49 – white

d What position will the 25th red counter be?

e What position will the 25th white counter be?

B2

● ● ● ○ ○ ● ● ● ● ○ ○ ● ● ● ● ○ ○ ● ● ● ●

Look at this sequence.

Repeat the questions in B1.

C1 You need a calculator.

a Choose any 2-digit number.
Reverse the digits.
Add both numbers.
Divide by 11.
Find the digital sum of the number you started with.

Example
   58
 + 85
 ───
  143
   13
5 + 8 = 13

b Do **a** 5 times.

Write what you find.

c What if ... you choose a 3-digit number?
Investigate.

Key idea | When you know your tables, you can spot the multiples of a number quickly.

N2 Steps and multiples

N2.4 Pairs of factors

> **Key idea** Every number has at least one pair of factors, the number itself and 1.

A1

x	1	2	3	4	5
1			3		
2	2	4			
3				12	
4	4				20
5			15		

You need squared paper.

Copy and complete the grid.
Find squares with these products.

4   6   8   12

Shade each set with a different colour.

A2 Find this square on your grid.
It shows 2 pairs of factors for 12.

```
     12
  2 | 4
  --+--
  3 | 6
     12
```

Find these squares on your grid.

a)
2	3
4	6

b)
3	4
6	8

c)
4	6
6	9

d)
4	5
8	10

Each one shows 2 pairs of factors for a different number.

Find the number for each square.

A3 Find the other pair of factors for each number in A2.

Write a factor sentence like this for each number.

The factors of 12 are 1 and 12, 2 and 6, 3 and 4.

Remember to check for all the factors systematically.

N2 Steps and multiples

B1 List all the pairs of factors for each number.

a 20   b 35   c 48   d 54
e 60   f 75   g 90   h 98

B2 Jack and Chloe have quick ways of multiplying 14 by 12.
They both use factors.

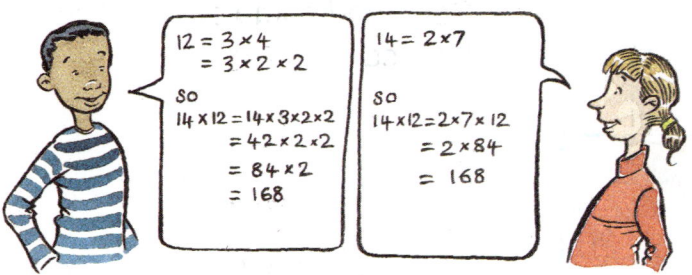

Use factors to find these products.

a 18 x 12   b 16 x 14   c 15 x 16
d 15 x 18   e 17 x 12   f 22 x 15

C1

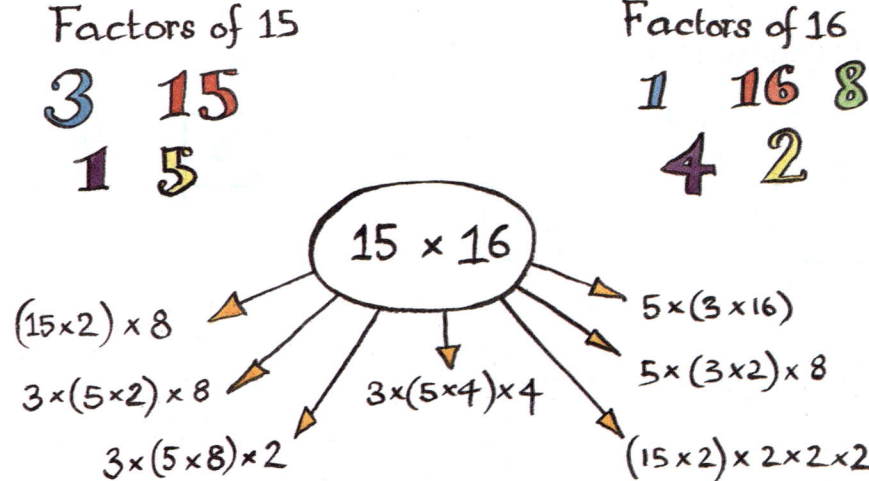

These are all ways to find 15 x 16.

a Try them all. Which do you like best?

b Do the same for 12 x 18.

C2 Do CM 19.

| Key idea | Every number has at least one pair of factors, the number itself and 1. |

N2 Steps and multiples

N2.5 Multiples of more than 1 number

> **Key idea** Most numbers are multiples of more than 1 number.

A1 Two circus fleas start at zero on a race track.

One flea makes jumps of 3.

The other flea makes jumps of 5.

Write the numbers up to 50 that both fleas land on.

A2
a Copy and complete this table.

b Every 2nd multiple of 2 is a multiple of ☐.

Every 2nd multiple of ☐ is a multiple of 8.

Every ☐ multiple of 2 is a multiple of 8.

c 16 = 8 × ☐   32 = 8 × ☐

16 = 4 × ☐   32 = 4 × ☐

16 = 2 × ☐   32 = 2 × ☐

multiples of 2	multiples of 4	multiples of 8
2	4	8
4	8	16
6	☐	☐
☐	16	☐
☐	☐	40
12	☐	☐
☐	28	☐
☐	☐	☐

B1 Write the numbers up to 100 that both these jumping crickets will land on.

a a 7-jump cricket and a 3-jump cricket

b a 5-jump cricket and an 8-jump cricket

c a 6-jump cricket and a 4-jump cricket

d a 9-jump cricket and a 2-jump cricket

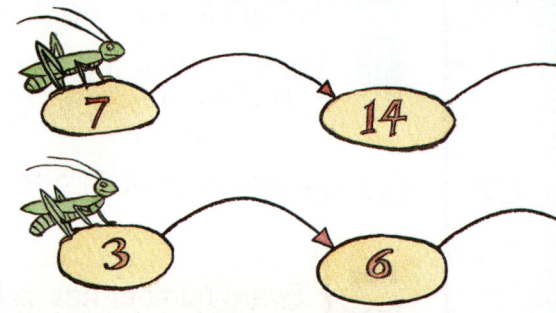

B2 Pat the ringmaster has 3 single-digit jumping crickets.
All of them land on all these numbers.

20   40   60   80   100

What size of jump does each cricket make?

B3 You need a 0–100 grid.
Use the clues and the 100 square to find the numbers.

a
My number is:
a multiple of 3, 6 and 2,
1 more than a multiple of 5
and also a square number.

b
My number is:
a multiple of 3, 4 and 6,
1 more than a multiple of 5,
a square number.

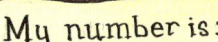

c
My number is:
a multiple of 6 and 7,
greater than 50,
3 more than a square number.

C1 Write 3 clues for each of these numbers

35   48   81

C2 List the numbers between 100 and 200 that are

a multiples of 2, 4 and 8

b multiples of 3, 6 and 9

c multiples of 5, 10 and 15

Key idea Most numbers are multiples of more than 1 number.

N2 Steps and multiples

N3.1 Making general statements

> **Key idea** You need to check any general statement by finding examples that match it.

A1
You need CM 67.

Find examples to match this general statement:

A number is not a multiple of 9 if its digits do not add up to a multiple of 9.

a Ring the multiples of 9.

50	51	52	53	54	55	56	57	58	59
60	61	62	63	64	65	66	67	68	69
70	71	72	73	74	75	76	77	78	79
80	81	82	83	84	85	86	87	88	89
90	91	92	93	94	95	96	97	98	99
100

(Multiples of 9 circled: 54, 63, 72, 81, 90, 99)

b Close your eyes and pick a number on CM 67.

c Is your number a multiple of 9 or not?

e.g. 83 is not a multiple of 9.

d Does your number have a digit sum that is not a multiple of 9?

83 : 8 + 3 = 11

e Repeat for 3 more numbers.

A2
You need CM 21.

a Play 'Four in a row' with a partner.

b Choose 3 different multiples of 6 from the game board and show how they match this statement:

A multiple of 6 is always twice a multiple of 3.
24 = 6 × 4   or   2 × (3 × 4)

Write your examples in your book.

You need a calculator.

B1 Copy and continue each pattern for 3 more lines.

Write a rule for finding the next line of each pattern.

Use a calculator to check your answers.

a 9 × 12 = 108

9 × 23 = 207

9 × 34 = ☐

b 12 × 9 = 108

123 × 9 = 1107

1234 × 9 = ☐

c 1 × 1089 = 1089

2 × 1089 = 2178

3 × 1089 = ☐

B2 Investigate these multiples of 9.

Look for the pattern in each part.

Write a rule for the next line in each pattern.

a 5 × 9 = 45

55 × 9 = ☐

555 × 9 = ☐

b 6 × 9 = 54

66 × 9 = ☐

666 × 9 = ☐

c 9 × 9 = 81

99 × 9 = ☐

999 × 9 = ☐

C1 Do CM 22.

| Key idea | You need to check any general statement by finding examples that match it. |

N3.2 Patterns and puzzles

Key idea | You can use what you know about patterns and number operations to solve puzzles.

★1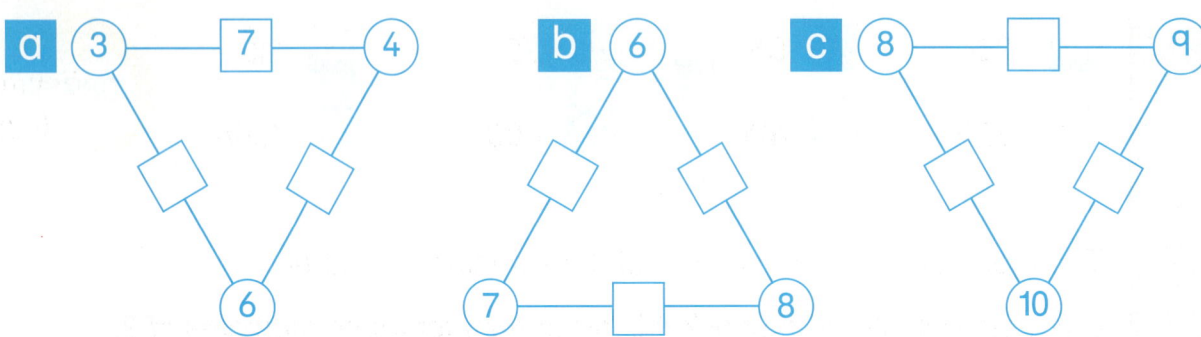

Look at the triangles.

The number in each square is the sum of the numbers in the next-door circles.

Copy each triangle. Fill in the missing numbers.

A1 The number in each square is the sum of the numbers in the next-door circles.

Copy the triangles. Fill in the missing numbers.

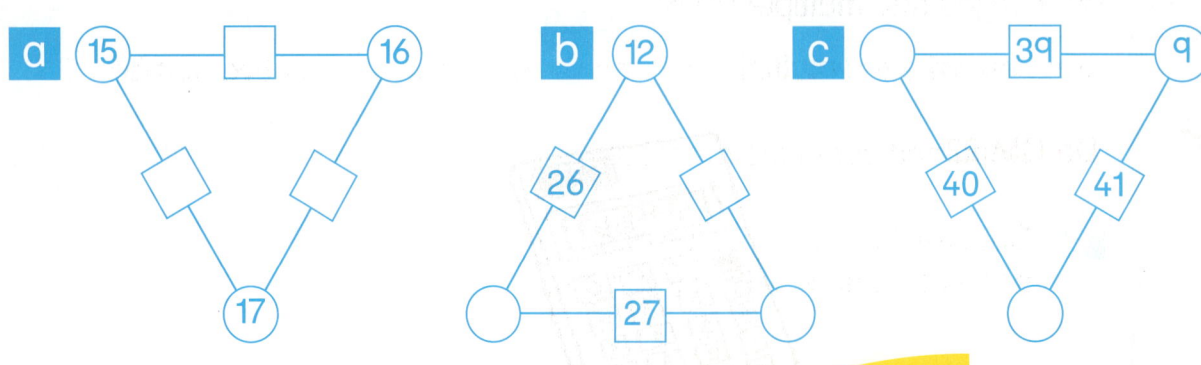

The numbers in the circles or in the squares are consecutive.

A2 Work out the 3 consecutive numbers that total the number in each triangle.

 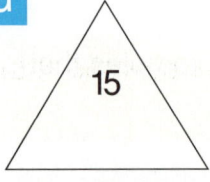 15    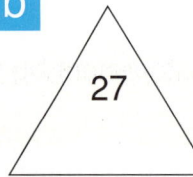 27   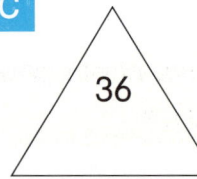 36   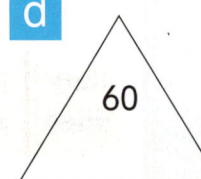 60

B1 You need a calculator.

The number above each pair of adjoining rooms is the product of the consecutive key numbers.

Find the consecutive key numbers for these pairs of rooms. Use a calculator if you like.

- a 30
- b 56
- c 72
- d 110
- e 380
- f 420
- g 600
- h 1056

Estimate first.

B2 The multiples of 3 are the sum of 3 consecutive numbers.

Use your calculator to check this statement for these multiples of 3.

Write a number sentence for each one.

- a 24
- b 39
- c 48
- d 123
- e 300
- f 162
- g 222
- h 204

B3 Look back at B2.

What if you had multiples of 5?

Can you write the multiples of 5 as the sum of 5 consecutive numbers?

a Copy and complete the table.

b Choose 5 more multiples of 5 and enter the results in the table.

Multiple of 5	5 consecutive numbers
20	2 + 3 + 4 + 5 + 6
35	
80	
125	

C1 Look back at B2 and B3.
Predict what happens for multiples of 7, 9, 11, ...

C2 Investigate multiples of 4.
Can you make a general statement for multiples of even numbers?

> **Key idea** You can use what you know about patterns and number operations to solve puzzles.

N3 Reasoning about numbers

N3.3 Factor puzzles

> **Key idea** Use what you know about factors and multiples to solve number puzzles.

A1 Find the pairs of factors for all the numbers from 10 to 20.

$$\text{e.g.} \quad 10 \ : \ 1 \times 10$$
$$2 \times 5$$

A2 Copy this table.

Use your answers to A1 to help you complete it.

Number of squares	Number of different rectangles
1	
2	
3	
⋮	
19	
20	

B1
a Choose an odd 1-digit number of squares other than 1.

b How many different rectangles can you make?

c How many different rectangles can you make if you have double that number of squares?

B2 Repeat B1 for 2 more odd 1-digit numbers other than 1.

B3 Look at your answers to B1 and B2.

a What do you notice?

b Does this work for all even 1-digit numbers and their doubles?

N3 Reasoning about numbers

B4 **a** Extend your table from A2 up to 25.

b Look at your table.

What number of squares gives you the greatest number of different rectangles so far?

c Why is this?

B5 **a** Find how many squares are needed to make exactly 5 different rectangles.

b Draw the rectangles.

B6 How many different rectangles could you make from 40 squares?

Use what you have found out so far to help you.

C1

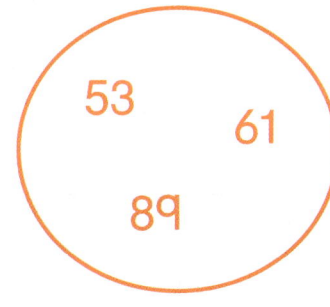

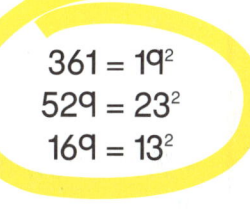

{ 53, 61, 89 }   { 361, 529, 169 }

$361 = 19^2$
$529 = 23^2$
$169 = 13^2$

a How many different rectangles can you make from 53 squares?

b Repeat for the other numbers in the sets.

C2 **a** Find 2 more numbers of squares between 50 and 100 that make only 1 rectangle each.

b Find 1 more number of squares between 100 and 200 that will make only 2 rectangles.

Key idea | Use what you know about factors and multiples to solve number puzzles.

N3 Reasoning about numbers

N3.4 Patterns and sequences

> **Key idea** When you discover the pattern you can continue the sequence.

A1 Copy and complete these sequences.

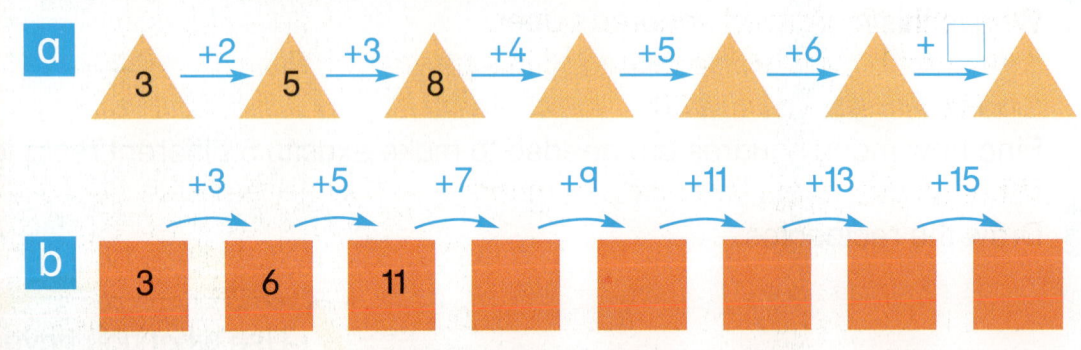

a) 3 →+2→ 5 →+3→ 8 →+4→ □ →+5→ □ →+6→ □ →+□→ □

b) 3 →+3→ 6 →+5→ 11 →+7→ □ →+9→ □ →+11→ □ →+13→ □ →+15→ □

A2 Find the 10th number in each sequence in A1.

Write in words how to find it.

A3 You need some counters.

- Make a shape with 5 counters. For example
- Grow your shape to make 5 more.
- Write how many counters in each shape.

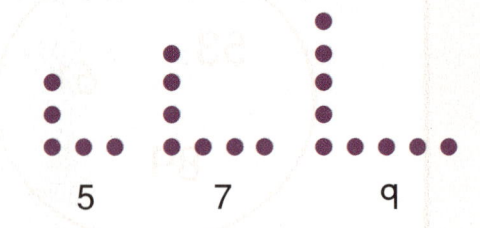

5   7   9

B1 For each sequence:

- Copy the diagrams.
- Find the pattern.
- Draw the next 2 in the sequence.
- Write the numbers.
- Describe to your partner how you knew how to draw the next diagram.

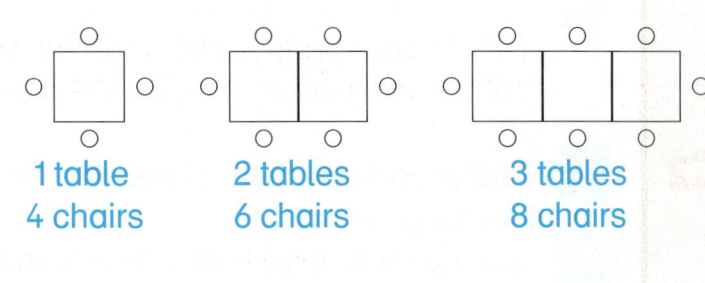

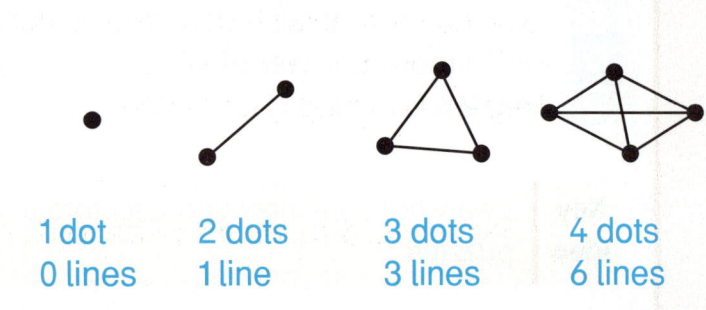

a)
1 table   2 tables   3 tables
4 chairs   6 chairs   8 chairs

b)
1 dot   2 dots   3 dots   4 dots
0 lines 1 line   3 lines 6 lines

40 N3 Reasoning about numbers

B1 **c**

5 dots

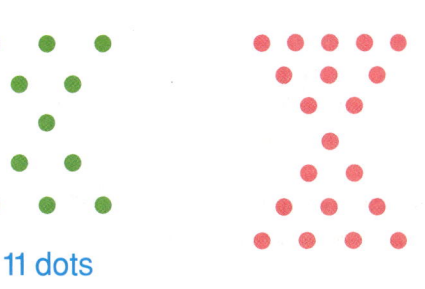

11 dots

B2 **a** Copy this diagram on squared paper.
The numbers 1 to 16 are arranged in a pattern.
Continue the pattern to 50.

1	2	5	10
4	3	6	11
9	8	7	12
16	15	14	13

b What do you notice about the numbers in the 1st column?

c What if ... you continue the pattern to 100?
Where will the next square numbers be?

Try to explain your reasoning.

C1 **a** Draw the next 2 shapes in this sequence of counters.

b How many counters will be in the 10th shape?

c Talk to your partner about all the ways you can think of to find the 10th shape without drawing the first 9.

C2 You need counters.

a Use no more than 8 counters to design a shape to grow.

b Repeat C1 using your shape.

Key idea When you discover the pattern you can continue the sequence.

N3 Reasoning about numbers

N3.5 Finding and using the rule

> **Key idea** You can find and use rules to solve problems.

A1
You need matchsticks and square dotty paper.

a Make each pattern with your matchsticks.

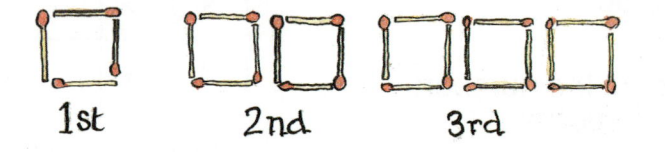

1st   2nd   3rd   4th   5th

b Make the next 2 diagrams in the sequence.

c Draw the 5 diagrams on square dotty paper.

d Count the number of matches you need for each diagram. Copy and complete the table.

number of squares	1	2	3	4	5
number of matches	4	8			

e Write about how the pattern works.

A2
Do A1 again for this matchstick pattern.

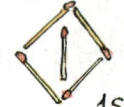

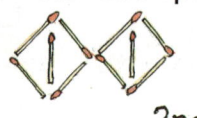

1st   2nd   3rd

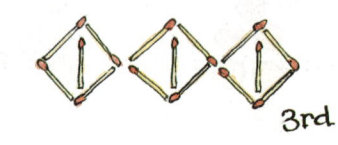

B1
Make these patterns with your matchsticks.

For both sequences:

- Draw the first 5 diagrams on dotty paper.
- Make a table.
- Predict the next 3 diagrams in the sequence.
- Discuss with your partner, then write a sentence for the function machine.
- Check your predictions.

a 1st   2nd   3rd

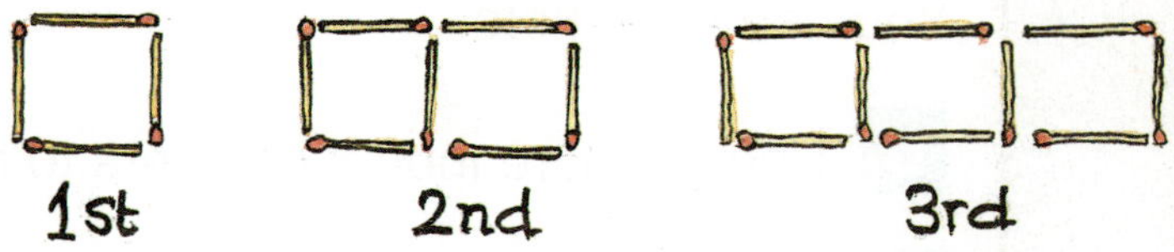

b 1st   2nd   3rd

N3 Reasoning about numbers

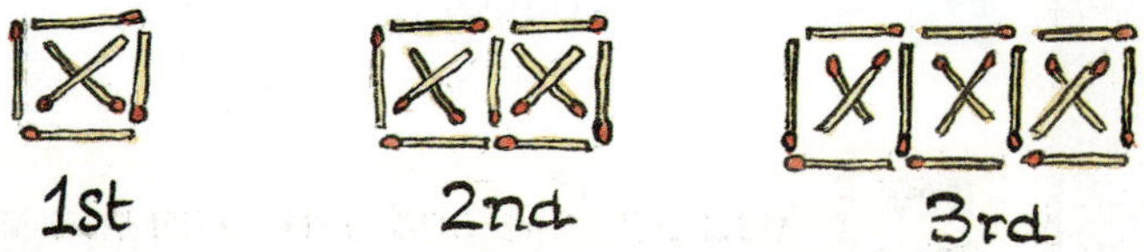

B2
- Draw the next diagram in the sequence.
- Make a table.
- Predict the number of matches for the 10th and 20th diagrams.
- Explain how you predicted the number for the 20th diagram.

C1 Investigate this sequence of squares.

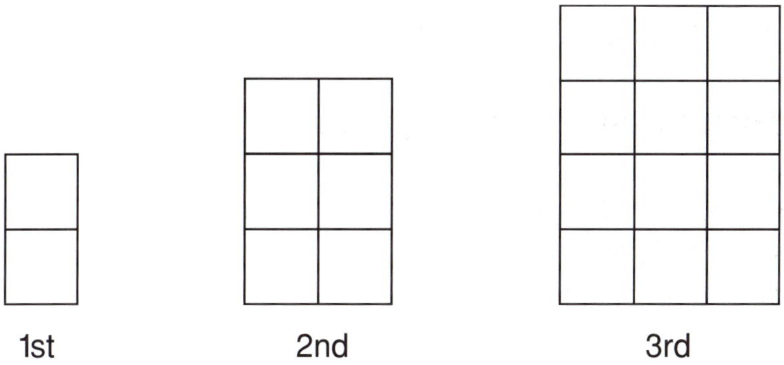

1st   2nd   3rd

- Draw the next 2 diagrams.
- Predict the 10th diagram.
- Try out some ideas for writing a sentence about the number of squares needed.

Key idea You can find and use rules to solve problems.

N3 Reasoning about numbers

F1.1 Equivalent fractions

> **Key idea** A half is equivalent to 2 quarters or 4 eighths.

A1 You need CM 26.

    a Write on each piece what fraction of the whole it is.

    b Colour in half of each strip.

A2 Copy and complete. Use CM 26 to help you.

    a $\frac{1}{2} = \frac{\square}{4}$ **b** $\frac{1}{2} = \frac{\square}{6}$ **c** $\frac{1}{2} = \frac{\square}{8}$

    d $\frac{1}{2} = \frac{\square}{10}$ **e** $\frac{1}{2} = \frac{\square}{12}$ **f** $\frac{1}{2} = \frac{\square}{16}$

A3 Look at your answers to A2.

    a Write down any patterns that you see.

    b Complete this. $\frac{1}{2} = \frac{\square}{14}$

    c Complete this. $\frac{1}{2} = \frac{\square}{18}$

    d Explain your answers to **b** and **c**.

A4 Make up 2 different equivalents of $\frac{1}{2}$.

B1 You need CM 27.

    a Colour in one quarter of each strip.

    b Write on each coloured piece what fraction of the whole it is.

B2 Copy and complete. Use CM 27 to help you.

    a $\frac{1}{4} = \frac{\Box}{8}$ **b** $\frac{1}{4} = \frac{\Box}{12}$ **c** $\frac{1}{4} = \frac{\Box}{16}$

    d $\frac{1}{4} = \frac{\Box}{20}$ **e** $\frac{1}{4} = \frac{\Box}{24}$ **f** $\frac{1}{4} = \frac{\Box}{28}$

B3 Look at your answers to B2.

    a Write down any patterns that you see.

    b Complete this. $\frac{1}{4} = \frac{\Box}{32}$

    c Complete this. $\frac{1}{4} = \frac{\Box}{36}$

    d Explain your answers to **b** and **c**.

B4 Make up 2 different equivalents of $\frac{1}{4}$.

C1 You need a partner and 8 small pieces of paper each.

- Write a fraction on each piece of paper.
- 2 of the fractions must be equivalent to $\frac{1}{2}$.
- Both put down a fraction.
- The player with the larger fraction wins both pieces of paper.
- If the fractions are equivalent no one wins.

Key idea | A half is equivalent to 2 quarters or 4 eighths.

F1 Equivalent fractions

F1.2 Thirds, sixths, ninths

Key idea | A third is equivalent to 2 sixths.
Ninths and twelfths are smaller than sixths.

A1 You need CM 29.

a Write on each row what fraction of the whole each piece is.

b Colour in $\frac{1}{3}$ of each strip.

A2 Copy and complete.

a $\frac{1}{3} = \frac{\Box}{6}$ b $\frac{1}{3} = \frac{\Box}{9}$ c $\frac{1}{3} = \frac{\Box}{12}$

d $\frac{1}{3} = \frac{\Box}{15}$ e $\frac{1}{3} = \frac{\Box}{18}$ f $\frac{1}{3} = \frac{\Box}{21}$

g $\frac{1}{3} = \frac{\Box}{24}$ h $\frac{1}{3} = \frac{\Box}{27}$ i $\frac{1}{3} = \frac{\Box}{30}$

A3 Make up 2 new equivalents of $\frac{1}{3}$.

B1

Copy the number line and put these fractions on it in the correct places.

$\frac{5}{6}$ $\frac{2}{3}$ $\frac{1}{6}$ $\frac{1}{2}$ $\frac{1}{3}$

B2 Copy and complete these sentences.

a One sixth is a half of _____.

b Three sixths are a half of _____.

c Two _____ are one third of a whole.

d Three ninths are one _____ of a whole.

e Four _____ are one third of a whole.

F1 Equivalent fractions

B3 Put these fractions in order of size, starting with the largest.

Use a number line to help you.

a $\frac{1}{6}$ $\frac{1}{2}$ $\frac{1}{9}$ b $\frac{1}{6}$ $\frac{1}{4}$ $\frac{1}{12}$

C1 The hands of a clock have gone wrong and are stuck so that they mark out $\frac{1}{3}$ of the clock face.

Write down the pairs of numbers they could be pointing to.

C2 What if the hands mark out $\frac{1}{6}$ of the clock face?

Write down the pairs of numbers they could be pointing to.

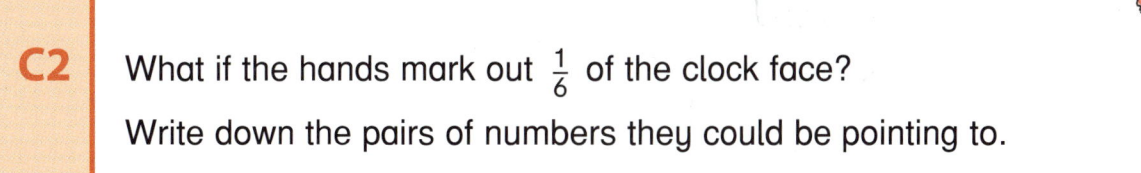

C3 Repeat for twelfths.

> **Key idea** A third is equivalent to 2 sixths.
> Ninths and twelfths are smaller than sixths.

F1 Equivalent fractions

47

F1.4 Tenths and hundredths

Key idea | One tenth is equal to ten hundredths.

★1

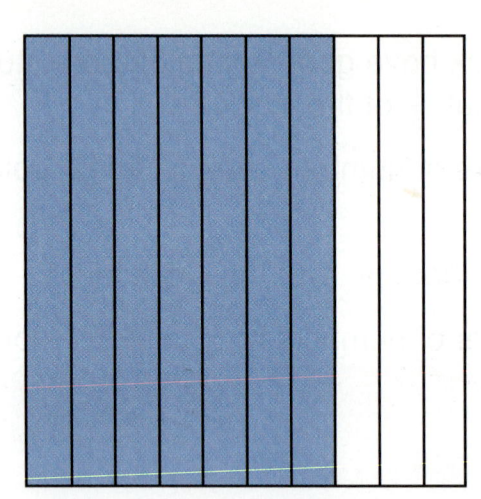

$\frac{7}{10}$ or 0.7 of this shape is shaded.

Each of these shapes has been divided into tenths. Show in 2 ways what fraction is shaded.

a

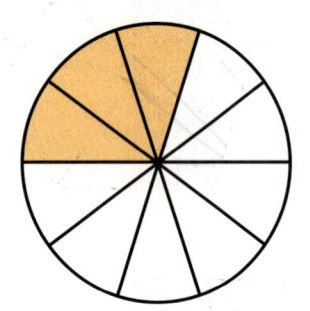

b

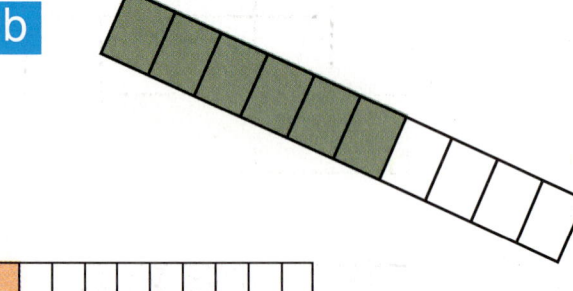

c

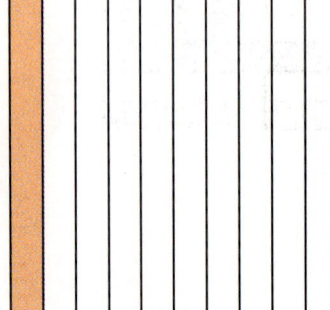

d

48 F1 Equivalent fractions

A1 Write the decimal that will balance each see-saw.

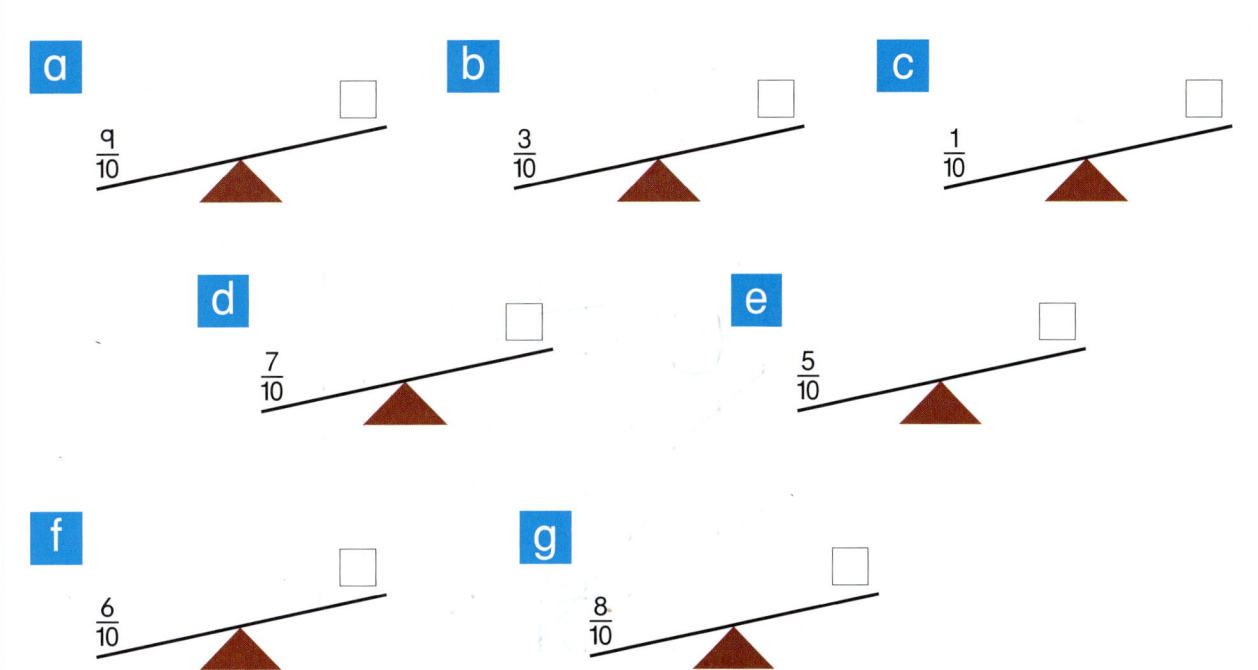

a) $\frac{9}{10}$ = ☐

b) $\frac{3}{10}$ = ☐

c) $\frac{1}{10}$ = ☐

d) $\frac{7}{10}$ = ☐

e) $\frac{5}{10}$ = ☐

f) $\frac{6}{10}$ = ☐

g) $\frac{8}{10}$ = ☐

A2 What fraction is shaded?

Write as decimals and as fractions.

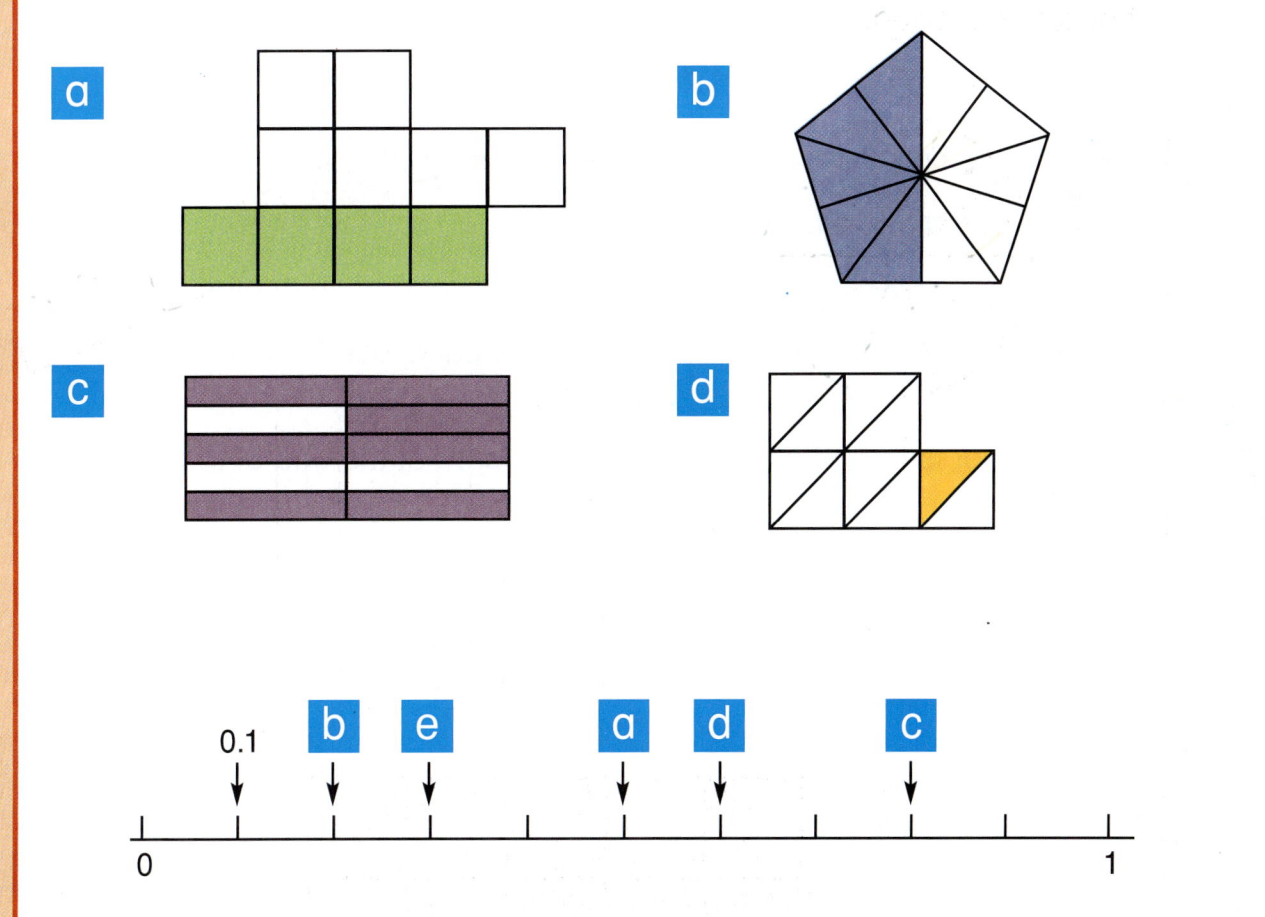

a

b

c

d

A3 The first arrow shows 0.1 or $\frac{1}{10}$. What do the other arrows show?

F1 Equivalent fractions

49

B1 Draw and complete the number line in $\frac{1}{100}$s.

$\frac{\square}{100}$

0 — $\frac{1}{10}$ — $\frac{1}{5}$ — $\frac{3}{10}$ — $\frac{2}{5}$ — $\frac{1}{2}$ — $\frac{3}{5}$ — $\frac{7}{10}$ — $\frac{4}{5}$ — $\frac{9}{10}$ — 1

B2 Order these fractions, smallest first.

$\frac{73}{100}$ $\frac{51}{100}$ $\frac{1}{2}$ $\frac{3}{4}$ $\frac{6}{10}$ $\frac{2}{100}$ $\frac{4}{10}$ $\frac{9}{100}$

B3 You need a partner and 2 sets of cards 0–9.

- Take it in turns to pick 2 cards. The first is the number of tenths and the second is the number of hundredths.
- Write your number as a decimal.
- Whoever has the larger number wins a point.
- The player with the most points after 10 rounds is the winner.

C1 You need the cards from CM 33 and 2–4 players.

- Shuffle the cards and spread them out face down.
- Take it in turns to pick up 2 cards.
- If the cards have the same value keep them and have another turn.
- If the cards are different in value put them back face down and the next player has a turn.
- The winner is the person who has most cards at the end of the game.

Key idea One tenth is equal to ten hundredths.

F1 Equivalent fractions

CM 33

F1.5 Improper fractions

Key idea | Fractions can be written in different ways.

★1 What do these pictures show?

a) 1 ▢/▢ apples

b) ▢/▢ apples

c) 2 ▢/▢ pizzas

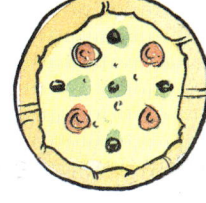

d) ▢/▢ pizzas

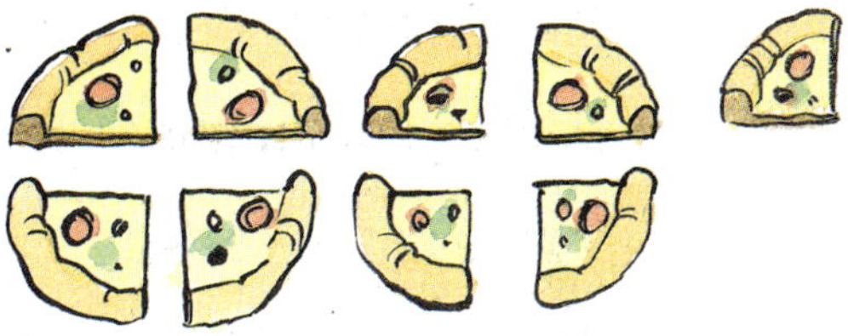

★2 There are 11 quarter biscuits on the table. They make $2\frac{3}{4}$ biscuits.

$\frac{11}{4} = 2\frac{3}{4}$

Write these fractions as mixed numbers.

a)

b)

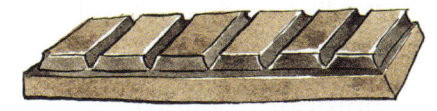

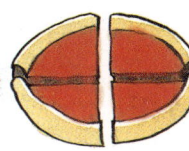

F1 Equivalent fractions

51

A1 What do these pictures show? Write your answer as a mixed number and as an improper fraction.

a

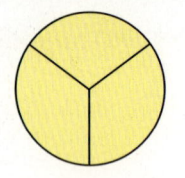

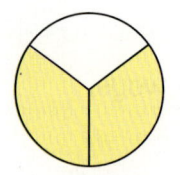

b

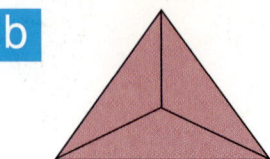

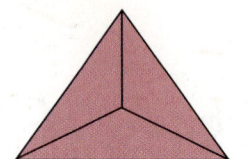

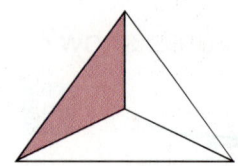

A2 a   b

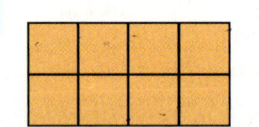

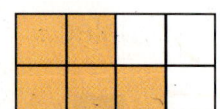

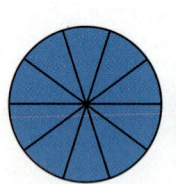

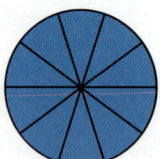

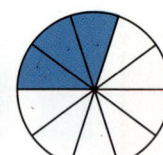

A3 a   b

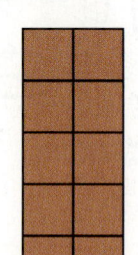

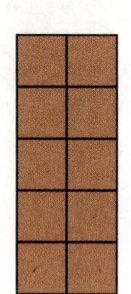

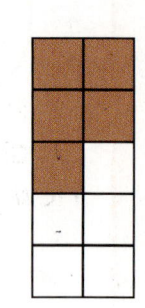

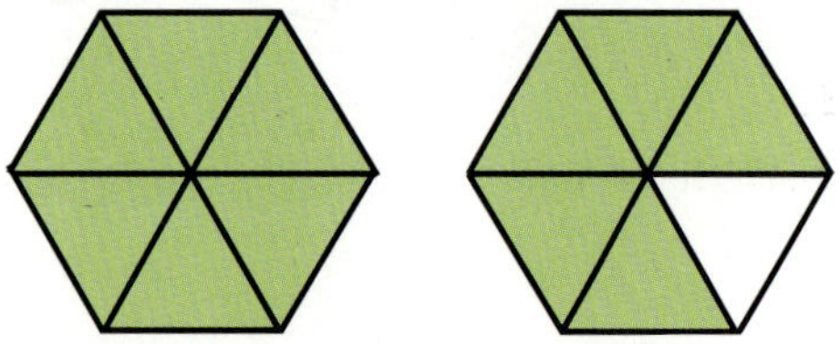

B1 Draw simple pictures to show:

a $1\frac{1}{10} = \frac{11}{10}$ b $3\frac{1}{5} = \frac{16}{5}$ c $2\frac{5}{8} = \frac{21}{8}$

B2 Write each of these fractions as a mixed number:

a $\frac{17}{10}$ b $\frac{13}{8}$ c $\frac{21}{5}$

d $\frac{7}{2}$ e $\frac{25}{4}$ f $\frac{16}{3}$

B3 Write each of these mixed numbers as an improper fraction:

a $1\frac{3}{5}$ b $2\frac{1}{2}$ c $1\frac{1}{6}$

d $1\frac{3}{4}$ e $10\frac{1}{5}$ f $3\frac{2}{9}$

F1 Equivalent fractions

C1 Each pizza was cut into 3 equal parts.
Sarah and her friend ate 7 pieces between them.
How many pizzas did they eat?

C2 The cafe sells mugs of hot chocolate. Each mug uses $\frac{1}{4}$ litre of milk.
How many litres of milk will be used for 29 mugs?

C3 Laura is making soft toys for the summer fair.
Each toy needs $\frac{1}{5}$ metre of material.
How many metres of material does she need for 17 toys?

C4 Food for the birds is sold in $\frac{1}{2}$ kg bags. The pet shop sold 33 bags.
How many kg were sold?

C5 Ben took part in a sponsored jog around a $\frac{1}{5}$ km path.
How far did he run if he ran round the path 16 times?

Key idea	Fractions can be written in different ways.

F1 Equivalent fractions

F2.1 Introducing hundredths

> **Key idea**   2 tenths and 5 hundredths is 0.25.

B1 Copy and complete.

a   7.51 = 7 + ☐ + 0.01   b   3.24 = ☐ + 0.2 + ☐

c   8.09 = ☐ + ☐ + ☐   d   11.64 = 10 + ☐ + ☐ + ☐

B2 Write these numbers as decimals.

a $\frac{3}{10}$ b $6\frac{7}{10}$ c $\frac{14}{10}$ d $\frac{4}{100}$

e $\frac{35}{100}$ f $\frac{62}{100}$ g $\frac{182}{100}$ h $5\frac{9}{100}$

B3 Write these numbers as fractions.

a   0.4   b   8.1   c   0.43   d   0.07

e   0.02   f   3.06   g   1.52   h   0.79

C1 You need a set of digit cards.

a   Pick 3 cards to make a decimal number to 2 decimal places. Write how many units, tenths and hundredths there are.

a   Rearrange the digits to make as many numbers as you can.

C2 Repeat C1 for 3 other choices of cards.

F2.2 Ordering decimals

> **Key idea** When you put decimals in order, begin with the most valuable digit.

★1 You need CM 37 and a number line.

Use the number line to help you follow each trail.

A1 Do CM 37.

A2 Put these numbers in order, lowest to highest.

8.63   9.45   3.11   4.31   6.82   5.72   4.04   7.29

A3 Put these lengths in order, longest to shortest.

3.41 m   5.39 m   8.59 m   9.64 m   1.87 m   4.86 m   7.59 m   6.24 m

F2 Decimal fractions

B1 Follow the decimal trails.
Each number in the trail is 0.01 more or less than the number before.
Record each decimal on the trail in your book.

a

start	4.11	6.41	7.93
7.99	7.26	4.12	8.26
6.32	4.13	3.86	3.54
5.01	3.22	4.14	4.97
5.19	4.83	4.15	4.16

b

start	8.79	3.46	5.01
9.78	9.79	9.8	9.81
7.44	6.03	5.99	9.82
9.86	9.85	9.84	9.83
9.87	8.88	5.55	10

c

start	3.46	3.45	6.54
9.01	8.63	3.44	7.99
1.42	4.43	3.43	4.32
2.37	3.98	3.22	3.42
7.36	8.94	1.56	3.41

d

start	7.01	9.44	10
8.25	6.91	6.92	6.93
6.97	6.96	6.95	6.94
6.98	8.75	9.65	9.46
6.99	7.1	7.11	7.12

e

start	5.71	5.7	5.69
6	5.66	5.67	5.68
7.01	5.65	3.51	6.75
9.46	5.64	8.71	10
6.49	5.63	8.24	5.63

f

start	8.01	8.02	8.03
3.42	9.04	6.57	8.04
8.99	7.99	3.57	8.05
8.08	8.07	8.06	6.75
8.09	8.1	8.11	8.12

B2 Find the missing numbers.

a 7.9 ☐ 8.3 8.5 ☐ ☐

b 5.6 5.9 ☐ ☐ 6.8 7.1

c 8.3 ☐ 7.7 7.4 ☐ ☐

d 3.9 3.4 ☐ ☐ 1.9 1.4

You need squared paper.

C1 Make up a decimal trail for a friend.
Each number must differ by 0.01 from the number before.

C2 Make up a decimal trail for a friend.
Each number must differ by 0.03 from the number before.

Key idea When you put decimals in order, begin with the most valuable digit.

F2 Decimal fractions

F2.4 Changing units

> **Key idea** It is sometimes useful to change measurements to a larger or smaller unit.

A1 A bag of potatoes weighs 4 kg.

Neil adds 1 more potato weighing 200 g.

How heavy is the bag of potatoes now?

Change measurements to the same units.

A2 John measures out 8.5 metres of string.

He cuts off 60 cm.

How much string is left?

A3 Parveen buys 5.5 m of material for her textiles project.

She needs another 30 cm to finish off the assignment.

How much material does she need altogether?

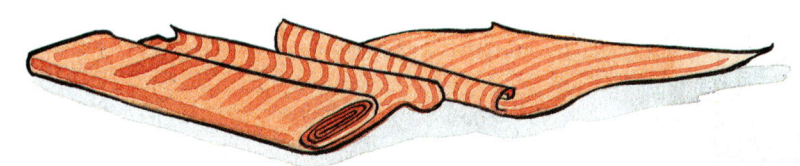

B1 Mr Cook took a new 10 kg bag of potatoes.

He used 1500 g of potatoes to make potato and onion soup.

How many grams of potatoes are left?

B2 We need 9 metres of fabric to make new curtains for the hall.

We need another 120 cm of fabric for tie-backs.

How much fabric is needed altogether?

F2 Decimal fractions

57

B3 13.5 metres of wire is made into paper clips.

Each paper clip uses 25 cm of wire.

How many paper clips are made?

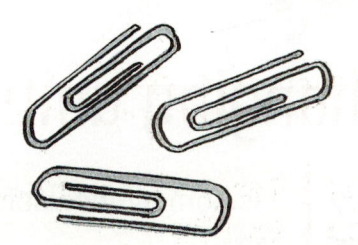

B4 A carpet tile is 50 cm long and 1 m wide.

How many tiles are needed to cover the floor of a hall, 6.5 m long and 1 m wide?

B5 Each clay pot uses 500 g of clay.

How many kilograms of clay are needed to make 12 pots?

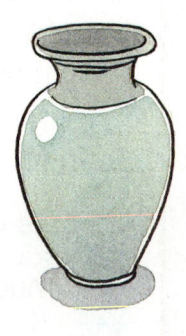

C1 Make up 4 problems of your own using mixed units of measurement for your partner to solve.

Use addition, subtraction, multiplication and division.

| Key idea | It is sometimes useful to change measurements to a larger or smaller unit. |

F3.1 Finding equivalents

> **Key idea** Tenths and hundredths can be written as fractions or decimal fractions.

Work with a partner.

1 Give the decimal equivalent of these fractions.

Example $\frac{1}{10} = 0.1$

a $\frac{3}{10} = \square$ b $\frac{9}{10} = \square$ c $\frac{5}{10} = \square$

d $\frac{2}{100} = \square$ e $\frac{46}{100} = \square$ f $\frac{99}{100} = \square$

g $\frac{8}{10} = \square$ h $\frac{80}{100} = \square$ i $\frac{75}{100} = \square$

j $\frac{10}{100} = \square$ k $\frac{6}{10} = \square$ l $\frac{4}{100} = \square$

2 Give the fraction equivalent of these decimals.

Example $0.5 = \frac{5}{10}$

a 0.9   b 0.03   c 0.52

d 0.25 e 0.66   f 0.07

g 0.7   h 0.11   i 0.01

j 0.35 k 0.05   l 0.6

3 Make up some examples of your own.

F3 Equivalence between decimals and fractions

F3.2 Calculator fractions

Key idea: $\frac{1}{2} = 0.5$; $\frac{1}{4} = 0.25$; $\frac{1}{10} = 0.1$

1 Work with a partner.

You need a 0–1 number line and a calculator.

Use a calculator to work out the decimal equivalent.

Mark the fraction above the line and the decimal below.

Example

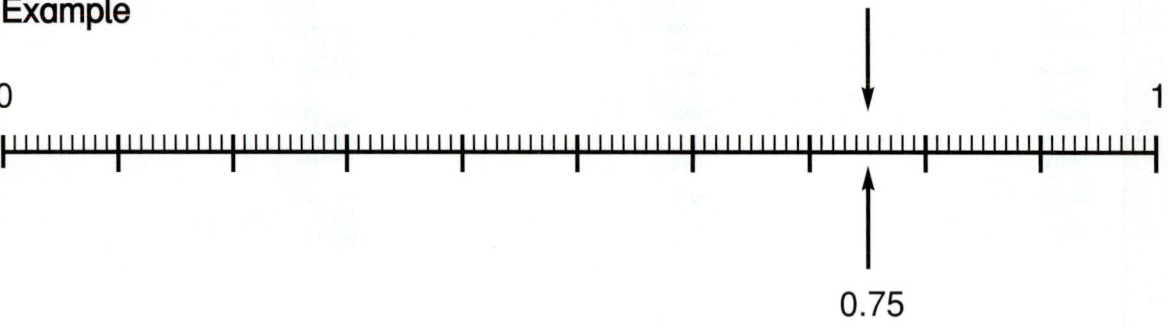

0 ———————————— $\frac{3}{4}$ / 0.75 ———————————— 1

- a $\frac{1}{2}$
- b $\frac{3}{5}$
- c $\frac{1}{4}$
- d $\frac{7}{10}$
- e $\frac{42}{100}$
- f $\frac{8}{10}$
- g $\frac{34}{100}$
- h $\frac{2}{100}$
- i $\frac{5}{8}$
- j $\frac{3}{8}$
- k $\frac{5}{9}$
- l $\frac{3}{20}$

If your calculator gives an answer with more than 3 decimal places just use the first 3 decimal places.

F3 Equivalence between decimals and fractions

F3.3 Decimals for money and length

> **Key idea** Centimetres can be written as decimal fractions of metres.
> Pence can be written as decimal fractions of pounds.

A1 Give the decimal equivalent of these measures and amounts of money.

Examples 83 cm = 0.83 m

45p = £0.45

- a 29 cm =
- b 50p =
- c 133p =
- d 105 cm =
- e 8p =
- f 7 cm =
- g 220 cm =
- h 425p =
- i 10p =
- j 75 cm =
- k 111p =
- l 60 cm =

A2 Do CM 44.

B1 Give the equivalent of these decimals.

Examples £1.07 = 107p or £1 and 7p

0.67 m = 67 cm

- a £1.25
- b £0.03
- c 1.43 m
- d 0.25 m
- e £0.84
- f 0.71 m
- g £2.02
- h 3.11 m
- i £0.10
- j 1.52 m
- k £5.55
- l 0.49 m

F3 Equivalence between decimals and fractions

B2 You need a calculator.

Total these shopping bills.

a
- bacon bites 67p
- jam tarts £1.58
- cheese roll 83p

b
- sherbert shimmies 23p
- yummy yoghurts £1.84
- sizzle sausage sandwich £2.26

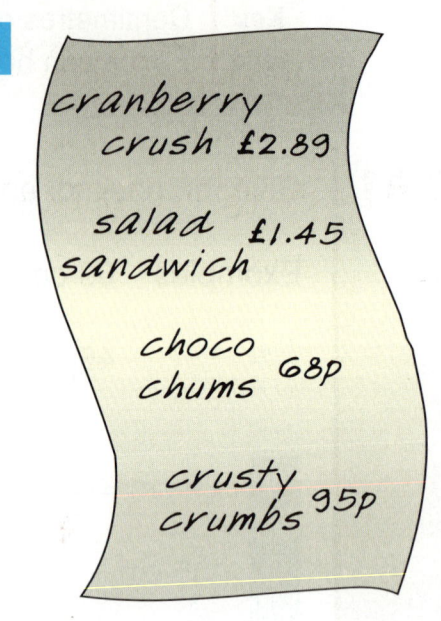

c
- cranberry crush £2.89
- salad sandwich £1.45
- choco chums 68p
- crusty crumbs 95p

C1 You need a calculator.

You have £4 to spend on lunch.

You buy 3 items shown on the shopping list in B2. You must buy a sandwich or a roll.

a You spend as much as possible.

What do you buy? How much change do you get?

b You spend as little as possible.

What do you buy? How much change do you get?

| Key idea | Centimetres can be written as decimal fractions of metres. Pence can be written as decimal fractions of pounds. |

F4.1 Comparing fractions

> **Key idea** You can compare 2 fractions and say which is greater or smaller.

A1 Copy and complete these statements about fractions.

Use > or <.

a $\frac{1}{4} \square \frac{1}{6}$ b $\frac{1}{9} \square \frac{1}{8}$

c $\frac{1}{5} \square \frac{1}{2}$ d $\frac{1}{3} \square \frac{1}{6}$

e $\frac{1}{4} \square \frac{1}{3}$ f $\frac{1}{6} \square \frac{1}{2}$

g $\frac{1}{10} \square \frac{1}{6}$ h $\frac{1}{8} \square \frac{1}{10}$

i $\frac{1}{4} \square \frac{1}{3}$ j $\frac{1}{6} \square \frac{1}{8}$

B1 Choose 10 pairs of fractions from the list to make up statements showing which fraction is bigger or smaller.

$\frac{3}{4}$ $\frac{1}{2}$ $\frac{2}{3}$ $\frac{4}{5}$ $\frac{3}{8}$ $\frac{1}{6}$

C1 **You need cards from CM 48 and a partner.**

- Shuffle the cards.
- Each in turn pick a card and then compare them.
- If yours is greater, you win both cards.
- If they are the same, you each keep your card.
- The player with the greatest number of cards at the end is the winner.

C2 With your partner, think of a new game that compares fractions and that you can play using the cards from C1.

F4 Ordering fractions

F4.2 Ordering fractions

> **Key idea** You can order fractions and compare them with $\frac{1}{2}$.

B1 Copy and complete these statements.

Use >, < or =.

a $\frac{1}{4}\ \square\ \frac{5}{12}$ b $\frac{8}{8}\ \square\ 1$

c $1\ \square\ \frac{8}{9}$ d $\frac{6}{8}\ \square\ \frac{3}{4}$

e $\frac{9}{8}\ \square\ 1$ f $\frac{5}{20}\ \square\ \frac{6}{10}$

g $1\frac{3}{4}\ \square\ \frac{15}{10}$ h $\frac{2}{10}\ \square\ \frac{1}{5}$

i $1\frac{1}{4}\ \square\ 1\frac{2}{3}$ j $\frac{11}{10}\ \square\ 1\frac{1}{2}$

k $\frac{7}{10}\ \square\ \frac{1}{2}$ l $\frac{4}{9}\ \square\ \frac{1}{4}$

B2 Copy and complete.

a $\frac{1}{2}\ \square\ 1\ \square\ 1\frac{1}{4}$ b $\frac{15}{12}\ \square\ 1\frac{1}{2}\ \square\ \frac{9}{4}$

C1 Copy and complete.

a $\frac{1}{8}\ <\ \square\ <\ \frac{1}{2}$ b $\frac{1}{2}\ <\ \square\ <\ 1\frac{1}{2}$

c $\frac{1}{2}\ <\ \square\ <\ \frac{3}{4}$ d $\frac{8}{9}\ >\ \square\ >\ \frac{2}{3}$

C2 Make up 3 number sentences like those in C1 for a friend.

F4.3 Ordering decimals

> **Key idea** Parts of a whole can be written as fractions or decimal fractions.

A1 Put the following decimals in order starting with the smallest.

a 0.9, 0.3, 0.1, 0.8, 0.5

b 0.75, 0.25, 0.5, 0.55

c 1.5, 2.0, 0.5, 1.0, 2.5

d 2.75, 1.5, 3.00, 1.75, 2.25

e 3.50, 0.35, 5.30, 3.05, 5.03

A2 Make up 3 lists of 5 numbers, starting with the largest number.

B1 Copy this number line.

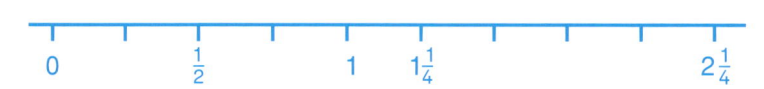

$$0 \quad \tfrac{1}{2} \quad 1 \quad 1\tfrac{1}{4} \quad 2\tfrac{1}{4}$$

Write these decimals in the correct places.

0.4, 1.8, 0.9, 1.6, 2.1, 1.2

B2 Copy this number line.

$$5 \quad 5.2 \quad 5.6 \quad 6 \quad 6.1 \quad 6.5 \quad 7 \quad 7.5$$

Write these fractions in the correct places.

$5\tfrac{1}{4}$, $6\tfrac{2}{3}$, $7\tfrac{1}{8}$, $5\tfrac{1}{10}$, $6\tfrac{3}{6}$

C1 Order these fractions and decimals largest to smallest.

a $\tfrac{7}{15}$, $\tfrac{1}{8}$, 0.3, $1\tfrac{1}{4}$, $\tfrac{15}{30}$, 4.6

b 0.5, $\tfrac{9}{4}$, 1.9, $\tfrac{7}{8}$, $\tfrac{10}{12}$, 0.2

c 3.1, 5.8, $6\tfrac{3}{4}$, $\tfrac{20}{2}$, 4.8, $\tfrac{6}{3}$

C2 Make up 2 lists of 6 fractions and decimals, this time starting with the lowest number.

F4 Ordering fractions

F5.1 Fractions and division 1

Key idea: To find a fraction of a number first divide by the denominator. $\frac{1}{9}$ of $36 = 36 \div 9$

A1 Find

a) $\frac{1}{4}$ of 24
b) $\frac{1}{3}$ of 15
c) one sixth of 12
d) $\frac{1}{8}$ of 40
e) one tenth of 60
f) one third of £3

A2 What is

a) $\frac{1}{10}$ of 1 metre?
b) $\frac{1}{4}$ of 1 metre?
c) $\frac{1}{10}$ of £1?
d) $\frac{1}{100}$ of £1?

Use pictures or apparatus to help.

A3 Find

a) $\frac{3}{4}$ of 24
b) $\frac{5}{6}$ of 12
c) two thirds of 15
d) two fifths of 25
e) $\frac{3}{7}$ of 35
f) five eighths of 24

A4 What is

a) $\frac{3}{10}$ of £1?
b) $\frac{7}{10}$ of 1 metre?
c) $\frac{19}{100}$ of £1?
d) $\frac{80}{100}$ of 1 metre?

F5 Fractions of quantities

C1 Find

a) $\frac{4}{5}$ of 120 cm
b) $\frac{5}{6}$ of £240
c) $\frac{4}{5}$ of 1 m
d) $\frac{6}{7}$ of 2 m 80 cm
e) $\frac{7}{10}$ of £310
f) $\frac{5}{12}$ of 96 cm

C2 a) Copy this diagram.

$\frac{1}{2}$ of 24 = 12

$\frac{1}{3}$ of 24 = 8

$\frac{3}{4}$ of 24 =

b) Add more fractions of 24. How many can you find?

c) Repeat the activity with a different number. Can you find one that gives you even more fractions?

Key idea | To find a fraction of a number first divide by the denominator.
$\frac{1}{9}$ of 36 = 36 ÷ 9

F5 Fractions of quantities

F5.2 Fractions and division 2

> **Key idea** 4 ÷ 5 can be written $\frac{4}{5}$

A1
  a If I share 1 carrot between 5 rabbits how much will each rabbit get?

  b If I share 2 bananas between 3 children how much will each one get?

A2
  a Write 15 ÷ 3 in another way.

  b Write 20 ÷ 5 in another way.

  c Write 16 ÷ 8 in another way.

A3

There were 10 chocolates in this box. Kim ate 3 of them.

  a What fraction of the chocolates has Kim eaten?

  b What fraction of the chocolates is left?

A4
  a What fraction of this shape is green?

  b What fraction is white?

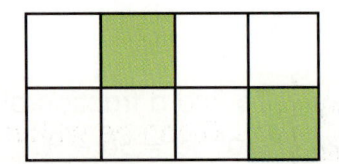

68 F5 Fractions of quantities

B1

a. 10 teachers share 3 apples. How much does each teacher get?

b. 7 elephants share 4 bananas. How much does each elephant get?

B2 Write each of these in another way and give the final answer.

a. $\frac{18}{6}$
b. $\frac{24}{8}$
c. $\frac{35}{5}$
d. $32 \div 4$
e. $36 \div 9$
f. $42 \div 7$

1 day = 24 hours.

B3 What fraction of 1 day is

a. 1 hour?
b. 6 hours?
c. 11 hours?

B4

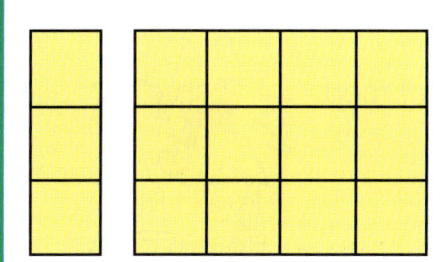

a. What fraction of the large shape is the small shape?

b. What fraction of the small shape is the large shape?

Key idea | $4 \div 5$ can be written $\frac{4}{5}$

F5 Fractions of quantities

F5.3 Problems involving proportion

> **Key idea** You can work out proportions to solve problems.

A1 For every bag of crisps I buy I get 2 tokens.

  a If I buy 6 bags of crisps, how many tokens will I get?

  b To get 8 tokens, how many bags of crisps must I buy?

A2 1 in every 3 squares in this pattern is purple.

  a Copy and complete: ☐ in every 3 squares are white.

  b Draw a pattern where 1 in every 5 squares is red and the rest are white.

  c Copy and complete: ☐ in every 5 squares are white.

  d If you draw 3 red squares, how many white squares will you need?

  e If you draw 16 white squares, how many red squares will there be?

B1 The local supermarket has a special offer for cat food.

  a Copy and complete this table.

Number of tins bought	Number of free tins	Total number of tins
3		
6		
	5	
	10	

  b Copy and complete.

  1 in every ☐ tins is free.

  You pay for ☐ times as many tins as you get free.

B2 Patti is making fresh orange juice. She needs 4 oranges for every $\frac{1}{2}$ litre of juice.

  a How much juice can she make with 8 oranges?

  b How many oranges does she need to make 2 litres of juice?

B3 A baby seal needs just 1 fish for every 4 its mother needs.

  a If the keeper gives the mother 12 fish, how many does she give the baby?

  b If the keeper gives the baby 2 fish, how many does she give the mother?

C1 At a sports club there are 4 boys for every 5 girls.

  a If there are 20 boys, how many girls will there be?

  b How many children will there be altogether?

  c If there are 20 girls, how many boys will there be?

  d How many children will there be altogether?

C2 **a** Design a pattern with triangles in which $\frac{1}{5}$ are black and $\frac{4}{5}$ are white.

  b Describe your pattern in 3 ways using 'for every' and 'in every' and 'as many as'.

Key idea You can work out proportions to solve problems.

F5 Fractions of quantities

F5.4 Quotients and fractions

> **Key idea** A quotient can be written as a fraction. $23 \div 4 = 5\frac{3}{4}$

A1
a. $13 \div 2 = \square$
b. $17 \div 2 = \square$
c. $11 \div 3 = \square$
d. $14 \div 3 = \square$
e. $18 \div 4 = \square$
f. $21 \div 4 = \square$
g. $28 \div 5 = \square$
h. $32 \div 5 = \square$

B1
a. $37 \div 4 = \square$
b. $35 \div 6 = \square$
c. $58 \div 6 = \square$
d. $19 \div 7 = \square$
e. $24 \div 9 = \square$
f. $48 \div 9 = \square$
g. $42 \div 10 = \square$
h. $99 \div 10 = \square$

C1
a. $60 \div 7 = \square$
b. $31 \div 8 = \square$
c. $85 \div 9 = \square$
d. $52 \div 7 = \square$
e. $70 \div 8 = \square$
f. $46 \div 8 = \square$
g. $47 \div 7 = \square$
h. $58 \div 9 = \square$

C2 Write divisions with the answer

a. $3\frac{3}{4}$
b. $2\frac{7}{9}$
c. $\frac{3}{10}$

72 F5 Fractions of quantities

F5.5 Quotients and decimals

> **Key idea**: A quotient can be written as a decimal fraction. 21 ÷ 4 = 5.25

A1
- a) 15 ÷ 2 = ☐
- b) 21 ÷ 2 = ☐
- c) 13 ÷ 4 = ☐
- d) 11 ÷ 4 = ☐
- e) 19 ÷ 2 = ☐
- f) 31 ÷ 10 = ☐

Remember to write the remainder as a decimal.

A2 Round these to the nearest whole number.
- a) 14.9
- b) 23.2
- c) 38.1
- d) 7.5
- e) 18.25
- f) 3.75

14.9 is between 14 and 15

B1
- a) 37 ÷ 4 = ☐
- b) 36 ÷ 5 = ☐
- c) 43 ÷ 4 = ☐
- d) 48 ÷ 5 = ☐
- e) 82 ÷ 10 = ☐
- f) 95 ÷ 10 = ☐

B2 Round these to the nearest integer.
- a) 19.7
- b) 30.8
- c) 25.82
- d) 71.08
- e) 10.50
- f) 82.49

B3 Round your answer to the nearest integer.
- a) 41 ÷ 4 = ☐
- b) 39 ÷ 4 = ☐
- c) 29 ÷ 5 = ☐

F5 Fractions of quantities

F6.1 Introducing percentages

Key idea: Parts of a whole can be written as percentages.

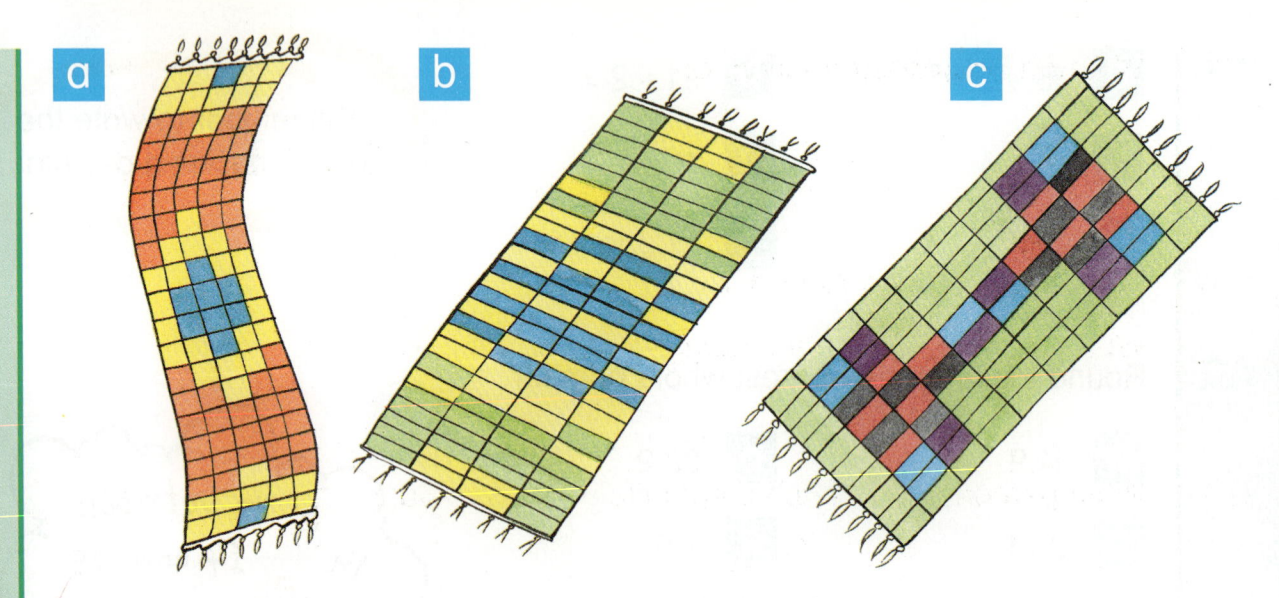

A1 a b c

Each carpet is made up of 100 shapes.

For each carpet write what percentage each colour is of the whole.

B1 Copy and complete.

a $\frac{1}{2}$ red = ☐ % red

b 10% yellow = ☐ yellow

c 25% blue = ☐ blue

d 100% yellow = ☐ green

B2 Use CM 60 to create a carpet with these colours:

25% yellow, 10% green, 25% blue, 40% white

C1 Copy and complete.

Carpet	Red	Blue	Yellow	Green
a	$\frac{1}{2}$	35%	10%	
b	40%		$\frac{1}{4}$	25%
c	10%		0	$\frac{1}{10}$
d		$\frac{1}{4}$	50%	10%

74 F6 Percentages

F6.2 Percentages of a shape

Key idea A whole item is 100%.
A half is 50%, a quarter is 25% and a tenth is 10%.

★1 Write an equivalent fraction for

a $\frac{2}{4}$ b $\frac{2}{8}$ c $\frac{5}{10}$ d $\frac{3}{12}$ e $\frac{2}{20}$

★2 Look at your answers to ★1.

Write the equivalent percentage for each.

A1 What percentage of each carpet tile is each colour?

a

b

c

d

F6 Percentages

75

A2 What percentage of each curtain blind is each colour?

a

b

B1 You need CM 61.

Design a carpet tile that has these colours.

a 25% red
   50% blue
   25% yellow

b 25% brown
   25% yellow
   25% blue
   25% white

c 10% green
   25% orange
   10% yellow
   10% white
   10% red
   10% black
   25% blue

C1 You need CM 62.

a Design your own curtain blinds using colours that are 10%, 25% or 50% of the whole.

b What fraction of the blind is each colour?

Key idea | A whole item is 100%.
A half is 50%, a quarter is 25% and a tenth is 10%.

F6 Percentages

F6.3 Percentages, fractions and decimals

Key idea | Parts of a whole can be written as percentages, fractions or decimals.

A1

a £8
b £24
c £32
d £28
e £36

YOU PAY 50% OF MARKED PRICE!!

How much do you pay for each rug?

FURTHER REDUCTIONS!

A2 The rugs are reduced again.

They now cost 25% of the original price.

How much is each rug now?

F6 Percentages

77

Ellie's electricals

SALE

- a: CDs £16
- b: £12
- c: £10
- d: £6
- e: £40
- f: £52
- g: £20
- h: £28
- i: £48 (computer games)
- j: £940

All radios 25% off
CDs 20% off
All computer games 10% off
computer 75% off

B1 How much do you save on each item in the sale?

C1 How much does each item cost in the sale?

C2 What percentage of the old price is the sale price?

Key idea Parts of a whole can be written as percentages, fractions or decimals.

F6 Percentages

F6.4 Percentage problems

Key idea | You can use what you know about numbers to find percentages of quantities.

A1 This table shows what carpets are made of.

Copy and complete it.

Name of carpet	Wool	Polyester
Hampshire	45%	
Yorkshire		27%
Highland	62%	
Essex	19%	

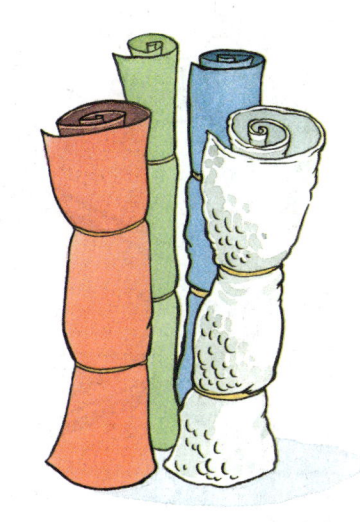

A2 What is

a 35% of 100 cm?

b 70% of £1?

c 15% of 1 m?

d 85% of £1?

B1 Use halving and quartering to find 75% of

a £300

b 500 m

c £800

B2 Find

a 10% of £3

b 10% of 11 kg

c 10% of 7 l

B3

a Paul got 45 out of 90 in his English test.

He got 45% in his maths test.

Which subject did he do better in?

b Meera got 80% in her English test.

She got 150 out of 200 in her maths test.

Which subject did she do better in?

C1 These rugs are in the sale.

Mr Major wants to make £1000 from selling them.

He will reduce prices by up to 75%.

Work out a percentage reduction and sale price for each carpet.

| Key idea | You can use what you know about numbers to find percentages of quantities. |